Experiments in Practical Spirituality

Experiments in Practical Spirituality

Keyed to *A Search for God,* Book II

by Mark A. Thurston, Ph.D.

A.R.E.®Press   •   Virginia Beach   •   Virginia

Printed in the U.S.A.

CONTENTS

Introduction: How to Use This Book

This is a book for individuals who are on a spiritual journey. If you are worried that perhaps this book is only for people who are in an *A Search for God* Study Group, please keep reading. This book has several ways in which it can be used. One use is as a supplemental aid to people in Study Groups working with .Book II of *A Search for God*. However, I expect that just as many people will read and use this book who are not currently able or inclined to join a group. The book is designed with the individual seeker in mind.

So what is this book all about? The word "experiment" sounds terribly scientific; and what does "cold, analytical science" have to do with spiritual growth? Admittedly "experiment" is a scientific term, but there is a difference between modern scientific *technology* (unfortunately, not too inclined to look beyond materiality) and the scientific *approach*. Basically the approach of science is to test things—to try them out—before claiming they are true.

In this sense we need to be scientific—with the Bible, with the Cayce readings, with the *A Search for God* volumes, or any spiritual teaching. We need to test the principles in daily, practical application. If we discover that a principle works and that it is applicable, then it is worth believing. That is what it means to experiment, and it can be done even with spiritual laws.

What this book presents to you is an orderly set of principles and theories to test. Some are going to work better for you than other ones. If you and a friend are both working with this book, you are going to discover also that different experiments work better for different people. In other words, even though we all live under the same universal laws, there is still uniqueness in God's creation. The same law applied by two unique souls may produce slightly different results. However, this fact should be exciting to us. It makes spiritual experimenting that much more diversified and open-ended than does experimenting with chemistry or physics.

One feature of this book which I think you will enjoy is the "bite-size" approach to learning and growing which it offers. A lot of people do not have time for more than five or ten minutes of reading a day. And many spiritually oriented books do not fit well into that sort of life style. However, this book is based on the premise that we can understand deeply only a few new thoughts at a time—not because of intellectual limitations, but because we have to live and apply something before we *really* know it.

And so, you will find nearly one hundred separate experiments in this book, designed to be read and applied individually. The reading will take only about five minutes. The applying may take a day for some experiments and several days or more for others. Each one will depend on how long you think *you* need to work with it before moving on to the next one.

The experiments are arranged in a consistent format. First is a quote from *A Search for God,* Book II. This quote will often state the essence of the principle or theory which the experiment will test. *A Search for God* was chosen as a starting point for each experiment for two reasons. First, I felt that this two-volume series is the most succinct statement of the spiritual growth philosophy of the Cayce readings, containing the essential ideas and hypotheses which each of us would need to try out and apply if we are to develop greater spiritual awareness.

The second reason for choosing *A Search for God* is that for a long time I have been impressed with the idea of a growth sequence in learning. That is how I learned mathematics, physics, chemistry and most everything else in school. Certain ideas can be learned only if certain other ones are learned first. Why would this not be true for spiritual learning as well? And *A Search for God* seems to be one attempt in spiritual literature to propose just what lessons in consciousness follow other lessons. By using selected quotes from ASFG I have hoped to recreate this quality of unfolding awareness.

After each of the quotes you will find an essay. Each essay is designed to expand upon and elucidate ideas from the ASFG quote. In some cases the essay draws heavily upon other Cayce readings; occasionally from the Bible or some other spiritual teaching. In many of the essays the ideas are my own.

Finally, each segment of the book ends with a specific experiment to be applied. Again, it should be pointed out that you must be the judge on *each experiment* as to the number of

2

days you will try to work on it. Those working on the book in a Study Group will find that the one week between meetings may work well.

I strongly encourage you to *keep a record of your experiences.* A spiritual growth journal is far more than just a diary of life activities. It is a record of *inner* events. Tremendous additional insights often come from a *process* of writing out feelings and new awarenesses. In *Experiments in a Search for God,* Volume I, I worded many of the experiments to say much more explicitly that I hoped you would record your progress and insights for each step through the book. It becomes redundant to use those words continually in each experiment, but please keep it in mind.

As you grow in awareness from applying these principles, I think you will discover that what we are doing is analogous to learning the use of tools. Imagine that you received as a gift a whole array of tools (e.g., drills, sander, power saw, etc.). You would need to learn to use each one individually. To do so you might focus for a day or a week on just that one tool, learning the range of its abilities and the subleties of its operation. This analogy is such a good one because it gives us a way of answering many questions and resistances which some people may have to a book like this one. I've worded them in terms of things you might hear yourself saying as you read this book.

1) "This experiment is crazy! If I did this experiment *all the time,* my life would be a mess." The key here is the italicized phrase. The experiment does not suggest that you will necessarily do any discipline all the time. It asks you to focus on a behavior or an awareness for just a few days. Suppose, in our analogy, that we could not hope to build nice furniture until we learned how to drill neat holes. We might spend a day practicing this procedure in different types of wood with different drill bits. Admittedly, just drilling holes will never get the furniture built, but it is a necessary skill to focus on temporarily. It is not an artificial exercise, it is a selective, focused effort for a greater purpose.

2) "I could never do all these experiments at the same time once I have finished the book. It would be too many things to remember, plus some of the experiments seem to run counter to other ones." However, do you use all your tools *at the same time* once you have learned the operation of each one? No, you use them selectively, confident that previous practice has shown you what the effect of each tool will be upon the wood.

3

Similarly, upon completing this book you will have an array of skills in consciousness to draw upon, using only the ones that are needed in specific situations.

3) "This particular experiment leaves me cold. I just cannot see how it fits my life." Certainly there may be a few experiments which do not fit your needs at this time. In our analogy, if you have decided that all you ever want to build is bookshelves, then you may feel no need to learn to operate a jigsaw. However, be very careful about writing off a particular experiment too quickly. Sometimes the very one we initially feel resistance toward is the one that will open up new areas of ourselves if we will persist through the initial confusion or boredom. For example, if I go ahead and learn how to use a jigsaw, I may realize that I want to build something besides bookshelves.

Finally, let me express how much I appreciate the encouragement I have received to write a companion volume to *Experiments in a Search for God.* The first volume was published in 1976 and in the intervening four years I have heard from literally hundreds of people who have read and applied the experiments in it. The fact that there is a second volume being published is evidence that this approach to spiritual growth has value and has worked for many people.

If you do not have a copy of *Experiments in a Search for God,* I think that you can feel comfortable in getting started with *Experiments in Practical Spirituality,* which you have in hand. Spiritual growth as a growth sequence is a bit different than mathematics or physics as a growth sequence. The latter is linear and the former is more or less circular (or should we say a spiral, because we *are* making progress, not just going around in circles).

With these words of introduction I now turn you loose in the laboratory of your own life. I invite you and challenge you to try some experiments—to test some hypotheses. Keep two helpers by your side as you work. First your sense of persistence. Certainly there are those rare moments of "eureka" in any scientific experimental endeavor. But behind those moments are days and weeks of persistent effort. And second, keep as a helper your own sense of humor. Experimenting ought to be fun and sometimes funny. I hope that you will have an open, anticipatory, joyful and playful approach to making the ideas in this book come alive for you.

Mark Thurston
February, 1980

4

Chapter One
OPPORTUNITY

"Opportunity is a material manifestation of a spiritual ideal." p. 3

To understand the principle of opportunity we must consider a pair of complementary concepts. First, that we all have ideals in life, even though we may not have considered them consciously. Second, that every event and challenge of daily living is specially designed and orchestrated to meet our individual needs in light of our ideals.

Too easily we fall into the following platitude, although admittedly it is with the best of intentions: "There are no such things as problems; there are only opportunities." Potentially this is true, but only to the degree that we actually know how to turn a difficult or challenging experience from stress or pain into discovery.

For example, suppose that I am out driving along a country road at night and get a flat tire. To my dismay I discover that my spare is also flat. Certainly this has all the makings of a "problem." Merely to repeat to myself the affirmation that "there are no such things as problems, there are only opportunities" makes neither my flat tire nor my stress go away.

How then do I meet this situation in the fullness of its potential as a chance to discover something? First I must see that this situation is not the capriciousness of fate or bad luck but that it has been specially designed by myself that I might know myself more completely. More specifically, the situation is a material representation of an ideal that I have held. But how could this be so? Who would hold as an ideal to be stuck along a deserted highway at night?

That, of course, is not what is meant. Rather there are several ways in which an ideal might contribute to creating this

5

experience. Recall that an ideal is that which is motivating and directing our lives. It is a spirit of living. Consider that we sometimes allow an ideal to control us in an *unconscious* way. Some opportunities serve to bring into consciousness an ideal which has been active yet not clearly recognized or appreciated. For example, if I have tended to ignore other stranded motorists in the past, I may not as yet have fully understood the implications of this neglect. Perhaps the current situation is a material manifestation of an ideal to which I need to face up and recognize. (In this case the word "ideal" is used to refer to whatever it is in a given situation which directs or motivates you. It may or may not be the highest or best one you could imagine. For example, we probably all have experienced incidents in which an ideal of self-gratification overrides an ideal of giving to others.)

A second way in which opportunity may be a material manifestation of an ideal is the challenge to apply what we have mentally set as an optimum ideal. If I have been praying to have greater trust in the Lord, then perhaps this will create for me physical circumstances in which I'll have the challenge and chance to live that way.

The example of the flat tire is perhaps very simplistic, but it serves to illustrate our first insight about opportunity. Knowing how to make a situation an opportunity instead of a problem *begins* by recognizing how our ideals have played a role in creating these circumstances.

Experiment: Try meeting each "problem" which confronts you in daily life with this question: "How would my own thoughts and ideals have played a role in helping to create this situation?" (Examples—(1) financial problem: perhaps past thoughts of fear about losing money created a self-fulfilling prophecy; (2) health problem: perhaps past attitudes toward my body led to poor eating habits and now this illness; (3) relationship problem: perhaps I have silently been overly critical of this person in the past.

"Each one of us is in a particular job, a particular home, a particular city, state and nation because he has prepared himself for this pattern. It is a time and place of our choice. We must begin our service here, now." p. 3

Restlessness is a quality which can especially undermine our capacity to recognize a situation as an opportunity. A mind which wanders to imaginings about hoped-for future changes is unable to recognize the chance for growth and discover it in the present. And so, a key to recognizing and using opportunity is the capacity to be in the now.

This is quite a skill because there are so many cultural forces that would teach us to be restless. If I have a cold, television commercials instruct me to swallow a few pills and avoid facing what my body may have been trying to tell me. Even the experience of being by oneself for a time is rarely tolerated in our society. We become restless in just facing ourselves, and a huge array of entertainment and diversions is all too available to us.

Paradoxically, when we resist the moment—when we struggle against the conditions which life has brought in a specific situation—that resistance serves to lengthen the experience. The old adage of "the watched pot never boils" is a psychological, if perhaps not physical, fact. When we resist the events of the moment we act to strengthen their hold and to prolong their existence. And this is far more than just the relativity of time which predicts that experiences we enjoy go by more quickly. Rather it is because there are lessons to be learned—opportunities which must be met.

If we resist recognizing the "opportunity quality" of a difficult situation and become restless, then it makes it all the more likely that the current conditions will remain until we discover what the situation demands. And even if we seem to be lucky and by our restless nature act so as to change the circumstances, we have no doubt insured a recurrence of the situation sometime soon. If I swallow pills to get rid of illness symptoms without taking time to listen and learn from my body, I insure that soon there will be a new illness. If I restlessly turn on the television to avoid dealing with how I am feeling today, I insure that just ahead there will be a circumstance to make me face that feeling.

Our affirmation can be, "I am in no hurry to have the present moment end—I want to experience it and know it as fully as I can." Such an affirmation invites the inherent opportunity for the learning and discovery which is a part of every moment to reveal itself.

Experiment: Whenever you find yourself restless or disenchanted with a current situation, become aware of how it has been particularly created for you here and now because it perfectly meets your need for that experience. Thank the Father for it.

"Through simple thoughts and acts we prepare for the greater opportunities that lie ahead of each soul." p. 4

No doubt we usually fail to recognize what is really important or what really counts in daily life events. Trained to measure greatness by appearances, we frequently miss the true opportunity of an event. But life in the earth is not at all what it appears to be. In fact it is only through doing the little things with love and awareness that anything lasting is achieved.

Those of us who are actively working on the spiritual path especially want to make a difference in the world. We want to be able to do things that will heal and bring greater peace for humanity. Yet seemingly it appears out of our reach to make much of a difference. Lacking the power base of a world leader, how can we have any leverage at all in the world situation?

For this kind of thinking, one of the most perplexing of all Biblical events is God's promise that an evil city would be saved by the righteousness of even ten people. Viewed by a strictly physical standpoint this seems absurd, particularly because even if Abraham would have found those ten righteous men, it would have been highly unlikely that they would have been leaders of the city. More likely they would have been humble and poor workers.

But a principle of this story is that there is in fact great power in "behind-the-scenes" loving. There is a power of mind and spirit to reach out beyond physical limitations and touch the lives of others, even without their knowing or understanding what has happened. Perhaps this principle is akin to a tuning fork, which after having been struck can also set other tuning forks vibrating. Perhaps in the smallest act of kindness and love we stimulate that same responsive chord in all of humanity.

The Edgar Cayce readings frequently pointed out to people the significance of the little things—that before any big things could ever materialize there had to be an attention to little things properly done.

Q-5. Please tell me why the big things I have worked on have failed to materialize. Wherein have I failed? How may I—

A-5. [Interrupting] For the little ones have not been kept just as close in touch with the development of things as should be. The big things will develop, the big things will come out for the entity. Keep the heart singing. Keep the face toward the light, keeping self in attune to that Oneness wherein all power, and all force, is at the command of the entity in applying those forces known within self to meet the needs of each and every condition.   39-4

David Spangler in his open letter to the spiritual community at Findhorn, Scotland, makes a similar point. Here is a group of people intent on making a difference in world consciousness. Even by appearances it seems that they are on the verge of something great. However, notice what Spangler suggests is the real work and the real purpose for this community:

"Thus, in demonstrating the everyday quality of the Christ, the mission of the community, as I see it, is to emphasize the quality with which it transforms the events of every day into meaningful reflections of a divine spirit in action, love in action, wisdom in action, intelligence and will in action. . .Each day, people in the community are meeting challenges, raising families, doing work, trying to grow, communicating, sharing, struggling, pondering, uplifting, living; individually and collectively these experiences are the strength and the invocation of Findhorn towards the Christ. The great event lies in the collective events that fill the lives of quiet, ongoing people who may never stand out or seem possessed of special rank or talent within the whole. . ."

(Spangler, *Reflections on the Christ,* p. 106)

To recognize and respond to opportunity we must have the greatest of sensitivity. We must be able to go beyond our cultural tendency for the grand achievement or impressive accomplishment and instead focus on the highest *quality* of response to life no matter how small or insignificant it may seem to be.

Experiment: Focus on doing the little things of daily life well and with love. Choose one "little" thing, such as beginning the day with a prayer of gratitude, smiling, offering to help another.

"If we do not watch ourselves and know that of ourselves we can do nothing, our life may become clogged with egotism, bitter resentment, petty jealousies, and evil thinking." p. 4

Our ability to surrender may often be a measure of how successfully we are able to meet an opportunity in life. For God to work through us we must learn how to let go. Teachings about the practice of meditation are particularly instructive on this point and very relevant, as well, if we remember that we want to develop a meditative consciousness toward all of life. In his book, *Creative Meditation and Multi-Dimensional Experience,* Lama Anagarika Govinda writes:

> "To make life great, we must not try to hold on to any of its momentary aspects. Even the functions of our body teach us this by reflecting the laws of life. Everything that we try to hold on to, be it air or food, turns into poison. Exhalation and elimination are as important as inhalation and the intake of food."
> (Govinda, *Creative Meditation and Multi-Dimensional Experience,* p. 191)

This willingness and capacity to release and let go must be coupled with a complementary principle. Before letting go and surrendering we first have to affirm that which is our ideal. Herein lies the difference between release and indifference. If I do not worry about a certain person or certain situation, is it because I have surrendered and released it to God or is it because I simply do not care that much about it?

The kind of release that allows God to work through us must be preceded by a conscious affirmation of what we believe in and what we seek. If I expect God to work through me to help you, I should realize that there are two ways I can prevent this from happening. The first way would be to release all thoughts and concerns about you without first having affirmed my desire for your well-being (in other words, this would be indifference toward you). The second way would be to have great conscious concern for your well-being but to end up worrying about you constantly rather than turning it over to God.

Experiment: Practice a sense of release, of turning things over to God. Ask for His help frequently. Do the best you can, but know (and live as you know) that by yourself nothing can be accomplished of real value. Write and use as needed your own "release affirmation" such as: "I release this person or situation into the hands of God, trusting that He will bring to both of us that which is most needed."

"Our so-called better judgment, from the material standpoint, may suggest that it is wiser to step aside and let it pass; for if there is to be a failure, it would be better for another to have the experience rather than have it ourselves." p. 5

What is it about ourselves that must be protected? The instinct of self-preservation is within all living things and yet perhaps there are times when the impulse to protect self goes beyond what is necessary. It may be required to protect myself from physical injury, but is it always necessary to protect psychological self-images which I have created? We might each ask ourselves, "How much time and energy do I invest in protecting certain ways of thinking about myself?"

For example, consider a person who has a self-image of being very poised and self-assured. No doubt he spends a considerable amount of energy making sure he is not placed in situations which would make him look foolish. Similarly, to a large degree we all are probably trying to work on a self-image of being a successful person (although our criteria for success will differ). To what degree then do we try to avoid situations in which there is the potential for us to fail? How much do we hold ourselves back and avoid risks that could lead to a failure or make us look foolish?

One of the joys of the spiritual path is that it frees us from such concerns about our own self-images. It is a mark of great psychological and spiritual maturity to begin to define oneself in terms of the *process* of what one is trying to do with his life instead of the *form* of what things look like. For example, there is great freedom in seeing oneself in terms of the process of making the effort to reach out and love, instead of in terms of the form of how things look. If my loving overture is rejected or belittled by another, how does that make me feel about myself? Can I hold to the self-image of one who cared enough to try to help, or do I become preoccupied with how foolish my seeming failure must have appeared?

A part of learning to truly meet the opportunities of life

requires the development of this kind of psychological and spiritual maturity. We must dare to *look* foolish or fail for the purposes of God's work through us.

Experiment: Do not let fear of failure deter you from doing acts of love or service which are in keeping with your spiritual ideal. Approach life with a boldness that is not afraid to appear foolish. Seek opportunities to risk. Affirm: "I am capable of doing well all that comes to me to do."

"Are we giving hope, faith, and comfort to those who have not had our opportunities?. . .Is our faith firm in what has been promised, and are we passing it on to others?" p. 6

Our work in the earth is not only to discover our oneness with God but also our oneness with the rest of humanity. We are a family of souls and there are responsibilities to be learned and to be accepted by being part of that family.

Certain archetypal or universal patterns of growth are met by all souls at some point in their development. Considering the soul that was Jesus to be a pattern for us all, one Edgar Cayce reading suggests that He faced every challenge and temptation that any of us face. Perhaps that is a part of what made Jesus so sensitive to the human condition.

There is certainly evidence to support the notion of a human family. We appreciate our commonality of experience with others. However, as is often the case, we know of a principle because we have seen it or known it through a negative application. In this case, the adage "misery loves company" says that when we are suffering we like to know that we are not alone in that current suffering.

This experiment, however, asks us to find a more positive or uplifting expression of this principle. Even though persons who are hurting may find some measure of comfort in discovering that they are not alone in their suffering, there can be much greater comfort in knowing that there is hope—that this problem can be moved through and the lessons learned. We have a "family responsibility" to give a sense of hope to people we see struggling with those of life's challenges and temptations which we have already faced.

It is important to remember, however, a proper way to assume that responsibility. It is not by making the person feel guilty or inadequate for still having the problem. (For example, "Oh, haven't you solved that yet? I had that problem but have already worked it through.") Nor is it to give advice. (For example, "I was faced with that difficulty once before and I can assure you that here is the way to solve it. . .")

Instead, what such persons need to hear first from you is simply that you care and that you can sympathize with their situation. Next, what they need is a sense of hope which you may provide. It is not so much hope that the problem will soon go away, because you cannot guarantee that. Rather it is hope that something good and useful can come from the challenge or temptation of the current problem. For example, you might be willing to share how a particular characteristic was strengthened in you by this situation when you faced it. The person may then ask your advice on what to do specifically, but make sure advice is *asked* for before you give it. Most often you will find that the gifts of sympathy and hope are all that person needs.

Experiment: Make special efforts to help others through opportunities for growth which you yourself have recently experienced. Do not be "preachy" but rather be supportive and help others have faith. Begin to pray regularly for such people. Call, write a note or offer in some loving way to be with your friend in his or her time of need.

"If we do good, good must return to us, for 'like begets like,' not as a reward, but as a result of law." p. 7

Here is a spiritual law; but we must be careful not to think that we can manipulate it and use it to fulfill just any desire. This law describes far more than merely actions, because it includes what is in our hearts as well. That is, it includes our purpose or motive. For example, suppose that I aid someone with a difficulty knowing that I am going to be needing help with something of my own soon. Is my attitude that I am now making an investment so that what I want will be forthcoming later? The purpose speaks louder than the action. Here is what I might expect in the future: Someone *will* be available to aid me, but he will be willing to help only if he is paid back in some way.

The area of personal finances is another one in which the application of this law can be illustrated. It is a principle of economic healing that one must give in order to receive. Because of this, tithing of our income is recommended. But what is our consciousness toward tithing? As we give that money, is it for the purpose of getting more back? What is in the back of our minds and behind our behavior? Most likely the economic healing does not work if our motive in giving is just to get more back. The trick is to give without thought of return—to find our joy in the very act of the giving.

On the other hand, when we do give with the proper spirit, the law works to bring supply back to us. But what is behind *how* the law has worked? It follows this principle: We draw to ourselves experiences to confirm or reinforce the consciousness we have developed for ourselves. For example, imagine a chart which listed all people's income from top (highest income) to bottom (smallest income). My position is likely neither at the very top nor very bottom—let us imagine somewhere near the middle.

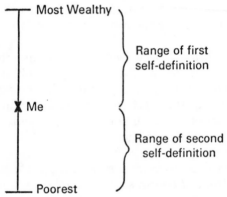

When I fail to give to others, I define myself in terms of those on the chart above me. I say to myself, "I'm barely making it; I cannot afford to give things away." I have a consciousness of being at the *bottom* of the segment of the chart; I define myself as poor, relatively speaking.

However, when I give to others who have less, I now am considering another segment of the chart and have defined myself as relatively well-off, when compared to those who have greater need than I. I have a consciousness of great supply and am likely to draw now to myself experiences to reinforce that consciousness. So it is not a cosmic accounting system by God of debits and credits but the simple working of a law of self-definition, consciousness and purpose.

As we try to live this law, remember it is not just with finances, but with anything we have to give, especially our love. The important corollary to this law is that the return of what we give very often *does not come from the same source* to which we previously gave. If I contribute $100 to a charity, I can hardly expect that charity to send me back $100 next week. In the same way, if I give love and attention to a person in need I should not expect that that person will necessarily be the direct source of what comes back to me. This sense of openness to give and receive from wherever it is offered is crucial. Too often we decide just how we want to be loved and by *whom,* and our rigidity may blind us from seeing just what is being presented.

Experiment: Do good for others but allow the good which by law will return to you to come from whatever source God chooses. Observe that it will not necessarily come back from the same person to whom you have done good. Keep a written account of unexpected good happenings.

"We must be in such close touch with the infinite source of understanding that we at all times may render the right service in the right place." p. 8

If love is infinite, then it not only reaches beyond boundaries of time and space but it also has unlimited modes of expression. We are constantly challenged to expand our notion of loving and to find new vehicles and modes of giving. Potentially we become *rigid* in our "loving" if it means that we think we have found the *one* way to give to others and that they must adapt themselves to it if they want to receive from us.

Probably we have all had the frustrating experience of having people insist that they love us and yet their way of loving does not fit our needs. The classic example of this is the "smother" type of love. Certainly the intention may be good but the way in which the love tries to express itself may not be appropriate or right.

Of course it requires the greatest of sensitivity to be able to "render the right service in the right place." But the first step is merely an attitudinal one on our part—a willingness to be open to discover new ways of serving and loving. Likely we insure that we will miss the spiritual opportunity inherent in a situation if we enter into it with a predetermined and rigid notion of how to love. Instead, our attitude and belief must be more like this: If I care about you and am willing to be really sensitive to you and listen to you, then I trust that your need will *draw out of me* the way of loving that you need.

This capacity to render the right expression of service is a key ingredient of "righteousness." Not only must our intention be correct but we must also be able to give in such a way that it meets the uniqueness of the moment. This is sometimes a scary business because, as with many things in life, we feel more secure with the familiar. And we all have several familiar and well-tested ways of loving and giving. However, our souls seek the *infinite* nature of loving. We can each expect to be confronted with situations which are opportunities to discover new avenues for service. The discovery comes from a sensitivity to what is needed by another rather than what we are used to giving.

Experiment: Be aware of how different situations and persons require different types of love and service. Try to be especially sensitive to appropriateness in your service to others.

"Have we had a cross to bear lately? If we counted it an opportunity, it was easier to carry. Maybe we learned just the lesson we most needed in this experience." p. 9

Sometimes in meeting a difficult life situation it may be helpful to remember that for the soul its experiences in the earth are dream-like. That is, the soul is "asleep" while in material consciousness and it might view daily life problems much as our conscious minds would deal with last night's dream. That is *not* to say that for the soul our daily life problems are a mere fantasy. Instead, it means that perhaps we can apply some of the tools of dream interpretation to our handling of a challenging waking life experience. Such an approach can oftentimes help us to perceive the opportunity which is present.

Most important is the use of symbolic images. We are familiar with how our nightly dreams portray parts of our unconscious selves in symbolic form. Has it ever occurred to you that in a difficult waking experience, perhaps you could try viewing the events, conditions and characters as symbols of the elements within your own soul?

Such a technique will be most helpful if we proceed to an overall view of the dream as did Edgar Cayce and Carl Jung.

16

That is, the notion that the dream has come to represent for us something which is trying *to be born* into our conscious awareness. Jung's very definition of a symbol points to this: the best possible representation of a complex fact not yet grasped by consciousness. In other words, the best personal image our unconscious could choose of some profound insight which has not yet been fully born into conscious awareness. The dream is a symbolic portrayal of a new kind of consciousness trying to be born. And notice how often that symbolic portrayal (i.e., the nocturnal dream) includes tensions, stresses or difficulties. Is it any wonder then that our waking dreams—which may equally well illustrate in symbolic form a new consciousness trying to be born—may be accompanied by feelings of confusion or stress?

This technique requires that you make a shift in perspective in viewing your life—that you consider the possibility that the same wisdom which produces your sleeping dreams may equally well produce planned waking dreams. Just as no nocturnal dream is interpreted by merely focusing on the painful or confused feelings in the dream, so we are challenged by this technique to discover what new state of consciousness these symbolic conditions are trying to draw out of us.

Experiment: Select a current difficult life experience. Write down in your journal: (a) exactly what is most difficult for you about this, (b) what new state of consciousness you are challenged to develop, and (c) what symbolic images you recognize.

Chapter Two
DAY AND NIGHT

"Through experience, through suffering, we come to know day and night, light and darkness, good and evil, even as the Son, the Adam. 'Though He were a Son, yet learned He obedience by the things which He suffered.' " p. 14

One rarely hears the word obedience any more. In a time of "doing your own thing" it is hardly popular. Perhaps we live in a period in which the pendulum has swung to an extreme position. For centuries the pendulum was at the other extreme. A false notion of obedience had been used to suppress aspects of the total person and to maintain authority and power over people. In reaction to this, at least in the Western world, we observe a celebration of individual authority and personal goals.

And yet within every soul there is an impulse to be obedient to something greater than oneself. There is a longing for certitude and authority and leadership. Something in us knows that we fulfill ourselves by obedience, but only if it is to the right thing. And that right thing must be spiritual law.

To the greater extent, the consciousness of humanity is not yet sensitive to or attuned to spiritual law. For example, Jesus presented a law which says that he who would try to save his life will lose it, and yet he who would be willing to lose his life for the work of the Christ would actually gain his life. However, we tend not to be sensitive to that law. Because there is a drive within us to be obedient to something, we tend instead to follow a law which says "save your own skin" or "the survival of the fittest."

The point here is that obedience itself is not the problem. We are already obedient because there is a natural instinct within us to be so. The problem lies in what we are obedient to. Too often lacking spiritual sensitivity, we forget or do not recognize the law which would make us happy and fulfilled. We end up faithfully obeying a law that considers only the ego or the material plane. We may like to think we are not obedient to anything—that we are our own person. However, such is not the case.

For example, if one becomes ill he must choose the law to which he will be obedient. Is it the law of oneness? That law would instruct one that body, mind and spirit are one, and that any approach to healing an illness must deal with spiritual purpose, attitudes, emotions *and* physical procedures. Or is he obedient to a philosophy of life and a law that considers only the material plane? Such obedience might lead him *only* to swallowing a pill to relieve the symptoms. The symptomatic relief may come, but misguided obedience has not led to a healing of the origin of the problem.

Even the Master Jesus had a final lesson in obedience to learn. Looking to His life as an example, we can see that it is not a sign of weakness to be obedient. It is not a denial of free will to be obedient to spiritual law. In fact the greatest joy and sense of freedom comes from using our free wills to shift from obeying the laws of selfishness to obeying the laws of love.

Experiment: Select a difficulty in your life or some situation with which you are struggling. Work at changing your attitude *by recognizing to what law it is* you must be obedient in order to move beyond the problem. In your prayers about this difficulty ask for a greater capacity to be lovingly and joyfully obedient to this higher law.

"But seek ye first the kingdom of God, and His righteousness; and all these things shall be added unto you." p. 14

There are three key phrases in the experiment as worded below. If we examine them more carefully in turn, it may make your work with this experiment more meaningful. (Skip down and read the experiment first.)

One phrase is "to be happy." We are happy when we feel a sense of fulfillment—when we have a sense of obtaining or reaching that for which we have been seeking. But that which we are looking for is within ourselves. The object of our longing and searching is in fact a state of awareness, a state of consciousness. The recognition of this principle is crucial if we are ever to be lastingly happy.

A second phrase is "need from the material world." Events, conditions, things and people in our outer, material world tend to stimulate within us particular states of consciousness. Seeing a person who I know loves me awakens in me a particular state of awareness. Entering a room in which I had a traumatic childhood experience tends to awaken within me a different consciousness.

The problem for us arises, however, when we begin to confuse the stimulus of the physical world with the response of our inner consciousness. I may begin to confuse the object or person of the outer world with the inner consciousness which it stimulates. I may begin to believe that I am powerless to bring forth that consciousness on my own and must have that person or object to do so. If the consciousness in question is that of happiness, then what I have done is to equate the person or object with my happiness. I have forgotten that there may be many ways in which that consciousness of happiness and fulfillment can be elicited.

This brings us to the third phrase, "to put God first." One of the great spiritual laws of the Bible is to seek first the kingdom of God and then all things will be added. However, many people understand this to mean that if they will put God first, then they will get a nice house, a nice car, plenty of money and so on. The problem with this kind of thinking is that they still are equating certain outer things with the consciousness of being happy. The law instead promises that if we put God first then we will draw to ourselves *whatever* uniquely matches our individual conditions so as to awaken a sense from within of fulfillment. A big part of putting God first is to give up our preconceived conditions of what it is going to take to make us happy.

Experiment: Tell yourself that for a week you will let go of anxieties about how you will obtain what you think you need from the material world in order to be happy. Make a special effort to put God first and be open to receive what He knows you most need. Affirm that you will trust God to bring you that you have need of.

"An examination of attitudes about material things, a critical study of personal ideals relating to possessions, will provide the solution." p. 15

In the Western world we live in conditions of relative affluence. That is, in the entire world which has so many people with little food, shelter or proper health care, we live with greater material blessings. How should we feel about this? What should our attitudes be toward blessings at a material level?

Some people in their compassion for those who are without material necessities have given up their own. They have felt that as long as they had material goods which so much of humanity lacks, then they could not be truly sensitive to the human condition.

However, others ask, "Did God intend us to inhabit the earth in poverty?" Are we to bring ourselves down to the least common denominator among all the people of the world in order to be fulfilling God's will? Perhaps we do the world more good if we give our bodies the best quality of food, shelter and health care we can, as long as it does not turn to greed or gluttony.

The resolution of any dilemma like this one involves an integration or balance between the two positions. On the one hand we do have a responsibility to those throughout the world who are suffering because of physical needs. We cannot write off the suffering of others by saying that it is just the karma of those souls to face such conditions. We must each find what is best for us to do to express our concern, be it financial contributions, involvement in social awareness programs or whatever.

At the same time, we need to be sensitive at a spiritual level to what is happening within those souls who suffer because of material needs. There is some degree of a lesson being learned. Things do not happen in material life in an arbitrary fashion. In a profound and even painful way many souls are learning a respect for the physical body. We all know this just from the experience of being ill. Once we move through the painful period and recover, we have a new respect and appreciation for the body and its care.

But, one might ask, in the case of persons who are hungry or sick or homeless throughout the world, what can *I* do? The money I might donate is well intentioned but seems to have so little effect that it leaves me feeling powerless to help. I understand that those individuals may be meeting karmic conditions they have personally built, but somehow I feel that I, too, have a responsibility in this situation.

Perhaps the answer lies in the very way we live with our material goods. If the healing of any condition must first happen at the level of consciousness only later to manifest materially, then maybe I can help the work of healing consciousness. My work may be to channel into the earth plane a greater appreciation for material things and their *proper* use in the spiritual life.

It may well be that all of humanity is in a kind of telepathic contact with one another, even unconsciously. Then breakthroughs in consciousness by even a few people may bring a certain vibration or consciousness into the earth plane and make that same breakthrough in consciousness *more accessible* to any member of the human family.

Suppose there is an individual on the other side of the planet whose soul is trying to learn the value and importance of proper, balanced nutrition. Perhaps that soul has chosen to learn in a painful and direct way by lacking proper nutrition. If I am my brother's keeper, what can I do to aid that learning process? Perhaps, to make financial contributions to food relief programs; but *also* to work on my own attitudes and consciousness toward food. As I take special care to put the best quality food in the proper balance into my body, then I channel into the earth plane a vibration and a consciousness that makes such an awareness a little bit easier for any soul trying to attain that awareness.

It is then our very attitudes toward the material blessings which we have that are tested. We can potentially use these material goods in such a way that they become a blessing for all humanity.

Experiment: Make a list of the major material things and possessions in your life. As a self-study, write next to each one your current *attitude* toward that material possession *and* what your ideal mental attitude would be.

Example: My house. Current attitude has been one of restlessness, wishing I had a bigger, nicer one. Mental ideal would be a sense of thankfulness and a desire to take really good care of the house I have, trusting that if it is best for me to move into another place, the way will be shown to me.

"Let us study to show ourselves approved unto our Maker, and not be confused, nor consider that the spiritual or mental

life is different from the material, but know that one is the reflection of the other." p. 15

It has become fashionable to be holistic. We have everything from holistic medicine to holistic parenting to holistic auto mechanics. One has to wonder not only what that term means but also wonder how many people using it have stopped to think very much about it.

Of course, the essence of the term is oneness or wholeness. However, the sense of oneness which a person has can go only as far as his scope or perspective on life. For the person who has only a physical point of view, his notion of holism or oneness might be to get all the physical ingredients working together. To a person who has considered the body and mind, holism would involve attitudinal and emotional ingredients. Such a person would not take physical actions (be they medical, parental, auto repairs or whatever) without considering the thought or feeling associated with the physical action.

It is perhaps unfortunate that so many people who use the word "holistic" limit its meaning by leaving out an active application of the spiritual component. Perhaps they find that thoughts and feelings are hard enough to get a handle on without trying as well to deal with purposes and motivations, which can often seem to be very vague or hazy. But to truly understand the operation of the body and mind we must make the effort to work directly with this spiritual dimension as well.

The point of this particular experiment is to have a personal experience of dealing consciously with holism. First we must differentiate holistic living from balanced living. To incorporate into my life a variety of spiritual, mental and physical disciplines is balanced living. For example, I might claim to have a balanced life if I meditate daily, record my dreams, get out in nature or in my garden, read a good book, do some kind of service for friends, exercise and eat a healthful diet. It is balanced, yes; but is it *integrated*?

The subtle but crucial distinction between balanced living and holistic living is the effort to work *simultaneously* with spirit, mind and body. That does not mean you have to be recording a dream as you jog down the street chewing on a sugarless, health-food protein bar. But neither does it mean that as you take your morning jog you are replaying in your mind an argument you had at work. An interest in balanced living too easily becomes a check-off list with which I can mislead myself about the depth of my accomplishments. The potential of a particular discipline is not fulfilled if, for example, I read my good book under poor lighting, sitting with poor posture, or if I eat that healthful diet but with a worried stream of thought and no sense of thankfulness.

Holistic living means working at all three at the same time. As I jog, I am clear about my purpose and ideal for doing this activity, *and* I hold in mind thoughts and feelings that will help to harmonize the three aspects of myself. As I eat that wholesome meal, it is with a sense of thankfulness to God and it is accompanied by thoughts which will help my body to assimilate properly that food.

When you first start the discipline of holistic living it is usually best to select just one area of your life in which to begin to practice the process. As accustomed as we are to compartmentalizing life, it may seem tricky at first—almost like learning to juggle three balls in the air.

Experiment: As all three—body, mind and soul—are important, so is it important to have a balanced, integrated life. Select an area of your life in which you need to have a better sense of working with all three aspects simultaneously. Try living that part of your life holistically.

"With the night, there comes to us an opportunity for rest, reflection, meditation and inspiration; or a time for sin, misery and mental torture." p. 16

How much do we value the sleep state and see it as an important part of our spiritual growth? Perhaps one way in which we can evaluate this is to consider how much time and energy we put in to preparing for sleep. This is not so much a matter of what we do before going to bed to insure that we will fall asleep quickly. It is rather a question of how activities before sleep influence what the mind will do during the following seven or eight hours. There is clear laboratory research to show that the mind is active throughout the sleep cycle, not just during the 90 minutes or so of dreaming.

A proverb that Edgar Cayce was fond of quoting says, "As a tree falls there will it lie." Some have interpreted this to mean that when a transition is made (such as the tree falling down), there is a directional quality to that transition and we are, so to speak, stuck with the results for quite some time. If this proverb is to be applied to falling asleep, it would mean that we should be very careful about the directional quality of the mind as we go sleep because to a large degree that will determine our mental activity for the next seven or eight hours.

Research has shown that the mind is highly suggestible in the hypnagogic state (that half-way state one passes through in moving from wakefulness to sleeping). However, it is likely that what we do with our minds in the 15 or 30 minutes before falling asleep is equally influential. Here is a straightforward experiment you can try. One set of variables will be presleep activities, the other set of variables will be the frequency and quality of dreams and your general mood and energy level upon awakening in the morning.

Experiment: Spend the 15 minutes before you go to bed on activities and attitudes which you feel will make it more likely that your sleep period will be one of rest and healing. Keep a record of these activities and the results.

Example: Pray, read poetry or inspirational material, sing, chant, etc.

"The night affords opportunity for us to appreciate the light; for hard experiences show us knowledge. Night is as a film upon which the real may be pictured. In this experience we may obtain a picture of the activity of light and become aware of whether we are making ourselves one with the light or are being held in darkness." p. 16

How is it that the night can be a teacher to us? If the very phrase "bring to light" means to understand, how can it be that darkness itself can also help us have insights into our nature?

Perhaps it is a question of relativity. It may be that what the ego or the conscious, waking mind experiences as darkness is experienced by other parts of the soul as enlightening. Consider the analogy of a lens to illustrate this:

Light which would have evenly illuminated every area of the concentric circles is now focused onto the inner circle only by the action of the lens. Point X is in a state of relative darkness. In our analogy the concentric circles are levels of the mind. The inner circle is waking, physical consciousness. Other circles

25

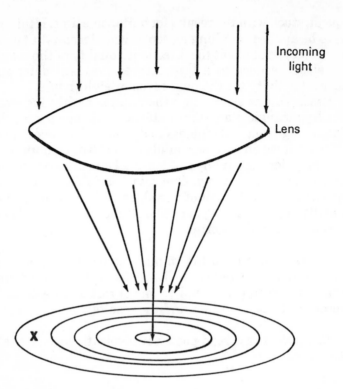

Incoming light

Lens

may represent expanded states of awareness to include forgotten childhood memories, past life experiences, telepathic awareness of others and awareness of the purposes of the soul.

The lens is a byproduct of incarnating. The fact that we have physical bodies serves to focus our energy and awareness in a limited fashion. But what happens when that body must rest and when we put aside our identification with the physical in sleep? In this analogy the lens is removed. Now all areas are potentially lighted.

This transition is experienced by the conscious mind as darkness, but only because of relativity. It is just as if you walked from bright sunshine outdoors into a dimly lit room like a movie theater. It seems to be total darkness. It is the relative quality of darkness that can make the dream or any encounter with the unconscious seem confusing.

However, if we can make the adjustment we can discover that this period of relative darkness is actually bringing into the light things which had been darkened before. There is no clearer illustration of this than in our dreams. The light of awareness shifts and no longer illuminates as intensely our sense of personal identity and physical life. But now, if we will pay attention, there is brought into the light hidden parts of ourselves. What we consciously experience at first as the night—as darkness—is, in fact, a teacher to us.

Experiment: Spend a week paying special attention to your dream experiences. Identify those elements of your dreams (symbols or actions) which reflect parts of yourself that you have been ignoring or have been darkened to you.

"What may we learn from the night? Have we built our night, or are we suffering that others may see the light?" p. 18

Just as the physical world around us is cyclical, our growth in consciousness is propelled forward by a rhythmic interplay of polar opposites. Time moves forward by the alternating current of day and night. Consciousness moves upward by the resolution and unification of polar tensions which have become painful.

To illustrate this consider the following diagram:

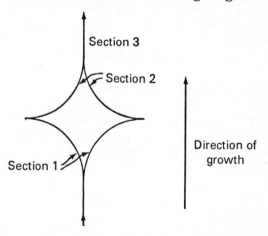

This depicts our growth in consciousness which is only occasionally linear and direct toward our ultimate goal. In section 1 there is a growing tension within us. Some polar opposite is coming acutely into focus. It could be justice and mercy, responsibility and freedom, or one of dozens of other polarities which life situations force us to confront.

27

But as the tension grows the condition becomes painful. One part of ourselves identifies more and more strongly with one side of the polarity and another part of ourselves identifies just as strongly with the polar opposite. We feel fragmented, confused and in a *darkened state.*

Then we finally reach a point of resolution. We may have been in section 1 for days or even years, but there comes a time of dawning. A dream comes, a friend says just the right thing, or one day we just know what we will have to do. Now we enter section 2 in which the energies of the polarity can be integrated. For example, we see how to be just *and* merciful, we see how to experience freedom *with* responsibility.

In terms of time, section 2 happens much faster than section 1. It is this rapid coming together that releases the energies that have been built up in section 1 and which can now propel us upward for a period of consolidated, unified growth for awhile (i.e., section 3). It is like a frog kick in swimming: the legs are moved apart and then in a rapid movement pulled back together, creating a powerful thrust forward.

The period we experienced as darkness was actually a necessary period of storing energy. Certainly it is possible that we may have prolonged its release, but every great soul who has achieved enlightenment has had these periods of darkness. When we recognize that this interplay of darkness and light is archetypal to human growth, it gives us great sensitivity and patience with our own cycles and those of others.

Experiment: Try relating to a specific dark, confusing or suffering side of your life in a new way. Nurture a sense of appreciation for difficult or confusing times. Try to step aside and observe things as part of a greater process and find yourself with more patience with others in their periods of darkness because you understand its role in the greater process.

Chapter Three

GOD, THE FATHER, AND HIS MANIFESTATIONS IN THE EARTH

"God is a Father only to those who seek Him." p. 23

A foundation stone of our faith is the promise, "seek and ye shall find." This affirmation can keep us going when we are frustrated with seeming not to make any progress. However, we might ask, "What is genuine seeking and how will I know when I have found?" Somehow the second half of this question just does not seem to be satisfactorily answered by the simple response, "You'll know when you get there."

Rather it may be that God has a unique way of meeting each soul. The fulfillment of our seeking may be determined by those special things which we have longed for most. In *Foundations of Tibetan Mysticism* Lama Anagarika Govinda provides a beautiful answer to what it is we will find at the end of our seeking. God will come as the specific *fulfillment* of what we have individually *lacked*.

> "There are as many infinities as there are dimensions, as many forms of liberation as there are temperaments. But all bear the same stamp. Those who suffer from bondage and confinement, will experience liberation as infinite expansion. Those who suffer from darkness, will experience it as light unbounded. Those who groan under the weight of death and transitoriness, will feel it as eternity. Those who are restless, will enjoy it as peace and infinite harmony.
>
> "But all these terms, without losing their own character, bear the same mark: 'infinite.' "
>
> (Govinda, *Foundations of Tibetan Mysticism*, p. 24)

Having gained a clue as to what we might experience at the

end of our seeking, we are still left with the puzzle of how to go about genuine seeking. If I am pushing myself and making hard sacrifices, can I be assured that the intensity of my seeking is sufficient? If I read many books and ask many questions, is this reliable evidence for the sincerity of my search?

What we need is an insight into seeking which helps us distinguish *mere actions* which appear to be seeking, from a *genuineness of spirit* which must be present if we are ever to find God. True seeking is characterized by creativity and release. Failure truly to seek is characterized by rigidity and unconscious habit.

The sobering—and perhaps at first discouraging—fact is that many things we have been proud of as our regular accomplishments in seeking God are far from that at all. Our spiritual disciplines may have become rigid and merely habitual (and, as we shall see in the next section, consistency and habit are not the same thing). The "old self"—the ego self—may actually *hide behind* or *protect itself* with so-called disciplines of seeking. We can use our dreams, not as avenues of honest self-examination and revelation, but merely as a way to try to confirm what we want. We can use our meditation time, not as a period of surrender, but as a quiet time to dwell on our problems or desires.

True seeking must include this quality of release or surrender. We cannot bring God down to our terms. Admittedly, once we attune ourselves to God we must try to express that experience in our material lives—but that is not the same as believing we can make the initial attunement and at the same time hang on to all the old patterns of our conscious thinking.

The creative moment—the moment of real seeking and some day even finding—is in surrender and release. What we sadly forget is that such a release is not just letting go of attachments to possessions or fame or people. It may also mean letting go of a rigid habit of how one tries to approach God. For God is a God of creation, of that which is continually changing and evolving. It is with that spirit of newness that we must meet Him. Take a serious look at the ways you have been seeking spiritually: the vehicles you use, such as your meditation technique, your diet and exercise, your reading material, the way you work with your dreams. How many of those ways have become mechanical—a form without a spirit of creativity? These are the ones you need to surrender. Simply keeping a check-off chart of having done these things each day has not necessarily gotten you closer to God.

This does not mean that if your meditation procedure has become a rigid habit you are to give up meditation. It means you release the mechanicalness and habit. You create a new procedure which can keep the spirit of your seeking alive.

Experiment: Make a list of ways that you seek God (e.g., meditation, prayer, dreams, physical attunement procedures, reading material, giving to other people). Select a category which you realize has become rather rigid or habitual—that is, much of the spirit and creativity associated with it is now missing. Try a new way or form or procedure for seeking God in that area.

"What are the manifestations of the Father? The fruits of the spirit. Gentleness, kindness. . .patience, hope, persistence, and—above all—consistency in thy acts and in thy speech." p. 24

In the last section it was suggested that consistency and habit are not interchangeable terms. To some degree it may be that the difference in these two words would distinguish the person who is finding joy and fulfillment in his life from the one who is unfulfilled and frustrated.

A key to the difference is awareness. Merely observing someone repeatedly doing something does not immediately tell us if he is being consistent or if he merely has a habit pattern. We would need to know where his awareness is focused as he performs this action. In most cases when we do something habitually our awareness is on something other than what we are doing.

For example, the first time I drive to my new job I am very aware of the new traffic pattern I encounter and each turn I must make. However, months or years later I most likely drive to work habitually. My awareness is elsewhere as I drive. It is the same with any habit. In fact we even have a standard apology for times when our habits get us in trouble: "Oh, I'm sorry. I don't know what I was thinking about. I just did it out of habit." However, it is this very separation of conscious awareness from action which can so often be at the root of an unfulfilled life.

So, if awareness is the key which distinguishes habit from consistency, we might well wonder what it is we are to be aware of. Is it just to be aware of what I am doing? That is a start, but consistency is really more than just that. It is awareness of the *purpose—why* I am doing what I am doing *and* awareness of *how* the thing that I am doing relates to the broader picture. Both ingredients are needed. The first means that I am keeping my ideal conscious when I am consistent. The second says that consistency is interactional and holistic; it considers how the action affects other systems or other people. To keep this second factor in mind, recall the other way we use the word "consistent." It means not only "repeatedly done" as in "consistent effort," but also "harmonious with" as in "his plan is consistent with our overall goals."

Consistency, then, is not just a matter of repeating something. In addition to a time component, there is a quality dimension. As both an analogy and a practical exercise to do, consider this procedure: With your eyes closed, be aware of your breathing for 25 consecutive inhalations and exhalations. The actual breathing is a repeated action we do all day long. But what happens if we try to bring awareness to what has been habitual? At first, there is a tendency to go back to repeating the behavior unconsciously. After eight or ten breaths you may find your mind wandering off to something else. However, keep trying to maintain your awareness. Sense the purpose for your breathing—its work to bring oxygen and the life force to all cells of your body. Feel the interaction between your own breathing and the flowings in and out of nature, between your own breathing and the rhythms of the universe. Many people would say that this very exercise in breathing is the first step of deep meditation. We might say that living with "aware consistency" is the first step toward the meditative consciousness in daily life.

Experiment: Practice true consistency in your relationships to self, others and God. Consider the things you do repeatedly—by habit—and try to bring conscious awareness to them: awareness of the purpose for which you are doing them and awareness of how the things you are doing relate to the whole. For example, on my drive to work in the morning I will be aware of people and places. I will be conscious of why I have chosen to go to the place of work which I do. I will be aware of the part I play in this rush-hour traffic and cooperate to help get people safely to work.

"Condemn not in words, in thoughts or activity, that you be not condemned. Be angry and sin not. Be patient, seven times seven forgive; yes, seventy times seven." p. 24

Most of us have trouble knowing what to do with our anger. It is frequently there, but we try to hold it in because we believe it is not good or spiritual to get mad. What is even more frustrating is that we have heard time and again that suppressed anger only ends up damaging ourselves physically. We may find only minor consolation in that Jesus got good and angry once. We are glad we can point to that example in cases where we are pushed too far and angrily flare up. But still, we may wonder why Jesus is recorded to have done that only once. He certainly had many other seemingly good opportunities but He acted in such a calm and patient way.

The philosophy of a healthy personality which we find in the Edgar Cayce readings certainly has a place for anger. Here are two often quoted passages concerning the importance of anger:

For, one without a sense of humor or the ability to get mad is not worth very much, yet one who cannot control same is even worse.

. . .It is like being angry. He that cannot be angry is of little worth. He that cannot control his temper is of less worth.

2576-1

Hold not malice, though easily ye may at times be angry—but sin not. Righteous wrath is a virtue, as well as is patience—for they must arise from the same influence, or from the same motivative influence in one's experience. 2635-1

But what is "righteous wrath"? How can we understand it to arise from the same source as patience? To answer this we must refer to our earlier study of patience in *A Search for God,* Book I. One of the great insights Cayce offered about patience is that it is *active* (see pp. 79-81 in *Experiments in a Search for God,* Book I). If righteous wrath comes from the same influence as patience, then perhaps the key is to act because of our anger. In other words, anger properly used (and actually needed) is that which will get us to *do something* in order to change what needs changing.

Of course we have probably all experienced acting in anger and making things worse. Instead, what may be needed is to act only at that point where we once again have a motive of love in the backs in our minds. It is a tricky balance. If I wait and do not act right in that moment when I am steaming mad, I may later feel better about the person or condition and then do nothing. However, with effort and patience we can learn to live by this affirmation: I act *on* my anger but *not in* my anger.

Experiment: Explore in your own life what it means to be patient and forgiving and yet still be able to "be angry and sin not." Act *on* anger instead of *in* anger.

"To know our relationship with the Father we have to pass often through trials and sufferings. That is not God's way of finding us, but our way of coming into realization that we are on the wrong road. All of our trials have been of our own making." p. 25

One of the potential pitfalls of working with the theory of reincarnation is that we can end up believing that God punishes us for previous wrongdoings. However, God's will is merely that we would learn and evolve in consciousness. The spark of divinity within each of us exerts this kind of influence; it puts us into situations where that learning and evolution can happen. Of course, there are a variety of ways in which we can learn a particular lesson or make a specific growth step in consciousness. This variety might be roughly divided into two categories or two principal pathways.

The first pathway is the way of suffering. Frequently this avenue of experience is created by an attempt to hold on to the previous ways while at the same time trying to evolve to a new awareness. Certainly a topic as broad as human suffering does not lend itself to simplified theories, but one way of viewing its origin is the conflict of two tendencies of mind and will. On the one hand there are influences and impulses to grow to a new level of awareness. On the other hand there are the old patterns. When we try to move to the new while still holding on to the old, there is the experience of suffering.

Consider, by way of analogy, that you are standing on one

bank of a river and you know to get across you will use a small boat. Beside you are numerous boxes and crates of possessions which you have acquired and to which you have grown attached. Even though you are told that the boat will not likely make it across with you *and* all your possessions, you may insist on trying. However, halfway across the river the boat begins to take on water and sinks. You experience suffering and difficulty in swimming to get across. For some individuals the conditions may prompt them to swim back to their starting point, leaving the crossing for later.

It is interesting to note that the experience in which Jesus seemed to suffer most involved a crisis in will. In Gethsemane there was the awareness of the movement in consciousness He needed to make; and yet, there was still the hope that perhaps it could be done while He retained the current conditions ("If it be your will, then let this cup pass from me").

The second pathway of learning and evolution of consciousness is the one Jesus chose—the way of service. Apparently the same growth and learning can take place in service to God and others as can take place through suffering.

An example may help illustrate how this could work in terms of reincarnation and karma. Suppose that 150 years ago a proud and cantankerous aristocrat died. In that lifetime he had been unappreciative and insensitive to his hired servants. Because of habit patterns built in that lifetime there were lessons to be learned. One of the lessons would be a greater awareness of the value and importance of how one human being can be of help to another. In the lifetime as an aristocrat that soul had had such help but had not appreciated it.

Now there are two pathways the soul can take to make that growth in consciousness. One alternative is through suffering. Perhaps in the following lifetime the individual is frequently ill and bedridden. However, the soul insists on trying to hang on to the old condition of being the one in charge with people waiting on him. Others take care of him, and through his suffering, perhaps he learns to appreciate the help he receives. The alternative pathway is service. Perhaps the soul chooses a career of serving others and learns to appreciate and enjoy helping others in this way. The lesson to be learned is the same no matter which pathway is chosen.

Finally, we should keep in mind that the karmic pattern is not broken simply with the insight, "Oh, now I can see what this situation is trying to teach me." We also have to live and put into action that newly learned awareness. At that point of applying and serving we may be able to shift our growth in that area of life from suffering to grace.

Experiment: Replace any thoughts that God may be punishing you or making you repay an old wrong, with the understanding that it is mankind that chooses the way of trial and suffering. Pick an area of your life where there tends to be some suffering on your part (physically, mentally, emotionally) and see if you can determine what lesson it is teaching you. Then see if you can find some way to put that lesson into application through loving and serving others.

"Man and God do not measure greatness in the same manner." p. 25

In our society greatness has become a confused term. Some have noted that the distinction between notoriety and celebrity has been lost. A great person may not necessarily be someone who has acted in a way we admire but merely one who has appeared on the national newscast. Frequently the designation of greatness seems somehow to be tied to that of power. Kings or generals have been called great because they had power over the lives of others.

But if we examine more closely this quality of so-called power, we may arrive at a clearer criterion for greatness—one which allows us to call even the most humble or apparently insignificant person great. Let us, for the moment, consider power as the capability to get things done. However, this leaves us with the question of *what* is it that needs to be done whereby we can measure powerfulness. If we have a material, three-dimensional view of life, then we see powerfulness in terms of being able to control dollars or oil or the mass media.

However, as soon as we admit that life has higher dimensional qualities, then our criterion changes. With a world view of four, five or even more dimensions, what is it that needs to be done? The coordination and integration of those dimensions. And so the truly powerful person—the one who is really getting things done—is the one who is drawing on the depths of higher dimensional life and energies. Simple love and patience and kindness get things done with energies just as real as any we know. Furthermore, because the higher dimensions are not limited by time and space, the overall influence can be tremendous. Probably the influences which are currently holding the world together are a handful of anonymous individuals scattered around the world quietly channeling into the earth plane energies to stabilize the animosities and stresses being generated by so many others.

To simplify this into a diagram of reduced dimensions, we can consider a drawing like this:

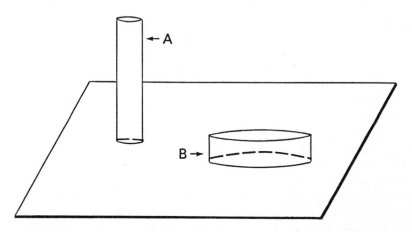

In our analogy the two-dimensional plane is the realm of material life. Person A has little extension of influence from a material viewpoint. Person B seems to have very extensive influence—what the newspapers might call a powerful person. However, as soon as we introduce the reality of a dimension beyond just material life, we see that person A is potentially getting things done which person B could never do. It behooves us, then, to keep sensitive to the deeper meaning of power. We can learn to measure greatness in the way God measures it.

Experiment: Observe how you evaluate the greatness of others. Work at recognizing and reinforcing (or reflecting) greatness in the lives of ordinary people who give of themselves and love.

"The Father has not left His children alone, but for every temptation has prepared a way of escape. Should we be less merciful? We were in the beginning made sons of God, yet few of us act as sons." p. 27

The classic problem for the spiritual seeker is temptation. This theme is found throughout mythology and sacred scripture. It is at the heart of the Judeo-Christian creation story and plays a key role in the preparation of Jesus for His ministry.

We all know the feelings related to temptation. It is the sensation of internal divisiveness. One part of ourselves wants to do something and another part says not to. Often the question we wrestle with concerns the identity of that second part. What is it that is saying no? Is it the God within, is it fear, is it memories of our parents' belief system? Because it can be such a difficult question to resolve, we often find ourselves in a dilemma in which we either feel guilty or repressed, no matter what we do.

As with most dilemmas there is no answer to be found at the level of the problem. Analyzing a tempting situation in the terms in which it has presented itself can rarely lead to a solution with which we will be fully happy. Perhaps we can look to the way in which Jesus handled temptation for an alternative method.

In the case of His three temptations in the wilderness, we have an especially clear example of the process of what happens when we are tempted. Temptation usually offers us the opportunity to use some resource which is available to us in a such a way that it will benefit only a fraction and not the whole. The word "fraction" most frequently means "only oneself." Jesus was tempted to use the great powers which He had in order to glorify Himself. Or, even more subtly, He had the option to use His great powers so that all the people *of His times* would believe in Him. And yet this might have kept Him from the way which would aid the salvation of *all souls in times to come.*

Jesus' response to temptation was to reaffirm His ideal. In other words He rejected one consciousness for another. He refused to adopt a kind of tunnel vision which would lead to very narrow benefits from the use of His resources. He chose to use the powers and energies available to Him to benefit the greater whole.

Perhaps we have in this example a pattern for meeting our own temptations. Rather than trying to determine the origin of the inner urge that says "don't" we can move to a new level of questioning. Ask yourself, "What should I do so as to benefit the most people?" Many individuals have found that for the behavior to cease they are able to give up an addictive habit only by seeing that it benefits others whom they love. Such addictive habits can be physical temptations (including food, drugs, smoking, sex, etc.); however, they can also include temptation to think or to feel certain ways (self-pity, worry, etc.). The answer to almost any temptation lies in our ideal to bring good into the lives of the greatest number of people.

Experiment: Select one area of your life in which you often feel tempted. It may be a temptation to act in a certain way or to hold particular thoughts or feelings. Try to look upon the situation as a way in which you are challenged: "Will you use the resources which you have available to benefit (or please) just yourself *or* yourself and others?" Then try to act in such a way that benefits are derived by the greater whole.

Example: When you feel tempted to eat more, consider how that resource can best be used to benefit the whole. If you are just going to eat to please yourself, then wait. However, if that food represents energy you need now in order to be about the work of living and serving others, then you have affirmed a purposefulness to your action.

"Here, then, you find a friend, a brother, a companion. As He gave, 'I call you not servants. . .but. . .friends.' " p. 27

Many of us can remember the childhood experience of making a new friend. There was excitement and a new world which opened up by having someone who liked us and cared about us, not because we were in the same family, but just because of the uniqueness of who we were. Friendship has that characteristic of life affirmation. Our friends are those who say, "I believe in you, not because I have to but because I want to."

This notion of Jesus as a friend is a new one for many of us. We can think of Him as an authority figure, but it seems quite strange to compare Him to the friend who lives next door. Hasn't Jesus been obliged to love us? Didn't God give Him this mission and wasn't He required to love us just as our parents loved us when we were children?

However, the Cayce readings' perspective of this soul we know as Jesus says that He knows each of us in our uniqueness.

It may boggle our conscious minds to think of actually knowing the specialness and uniqueness of billions of people, but the universal quality of the Christ Consciousness has unlimited specificity as well. In fact it was this nearly unimaginable quality of divine love which Jesus referred to when He said that not a sparrow falls but that God knows it.

So, Jesus who attained the Christ Consciousness is a soul who knows your soul and chooses to care about you in your uniqueness among all souls. He affirms what is good about you because He desires to do so, not because you merely happen to fall into some large category for which He has a responsibility.

However, that is just half of friendship. For friendship to truly blossom it needs to be a two-way flow. He needs us as well. His work in the earth needs us as workers. In fact the message is true for us today which was given long ago to Peter, perhaps Jesus' best friend in those times:

"When they had finished breakfast, Jesus said to Simon Peter, 'Simon, son of John, do you love me more than these?' He said to him, 'Yes, Lord; you know that I love you.' He said to him, 'Feed my lambs.'

"A second time he said to him, 'Simon, son of John, do you love me?' He said to him, 'Yes, Lord; you know that I love you.' He said to him, 'Tend my sheep.'

"He said to him the third time, 'Simon, son of John, do you love me?' Peter was grieved because he said to him the third time, 'Do you love me?' And he said to him, 'Lord, you know everything; you know that I love you.' Jesus said to him, 'Feed my sheep.' " (John 21:15-17)

Experiment: Try living your life as a recognition that you are Jesus' *friend,* not just an obedient servant.

Example: Be a friend to someone who needs a friend. Offer to go for a walk, have lunch with or simply listen to someone.

"What are the manifestations of the Father in the earth? To do good to all people, to manifest the fruits of the spirit in our thoughts and in our acts, as we meet our fellow men in their own conditions where troubles, doubts, fears and distresses assail them." p. 29

This passage from *A Search for God* challenges us to work with others in their own conditions of pain or trouble. And most of us find that in our lives we have taken on that kind of responsibility for a select number of people. We have friends and family members who know they can come to us for support and counsel if they are troubled. However, beyond the circle of these special friends and loved ones, there are those who neither expect us to be particularly concerned nor available for help when they have difficulties.

Admittedly, some of us have a very large circle and have this special kind of bond with many, many people. However, nearly everyone has drawn a line at some point. Certainly there are times when we must draw a line beyond which it is difficult to go in helping others, simply because of our own energy, time and health. But do we also draw a line, not because of limited time or energy, but because we do not want to have to deal with particular kinds of problems or people?

It may be very interesting for us to observe what kinds of people and difficulties we habitually avoid getting involved with. In some cases this may be due to the fact that there is a *part of ourselves* with which we have not wanted to deal. This does not necessarily mean that within us there is some hidden drive to get caught up in such a problem. For example, consider person A who avoids ever talking to or showing compassion for an alcoholic. That individual does not necessarily have repressed tendencies toward alcoholism. However, it may be that whenever person A has to interact with an alcoholic (even when in the sober state), there are certain feelings or self-images that come forth in person A which are uncomfortable. It is *easier* for person A to avoid merely ever trying to know and help alcoholics.

However, one of the growth principles in the Cayce readings says, "Truly therefore, in knowing self is knowing the other fellow also, for all are parts of one mind." (262-10) One application of this principle is that we can come to know, understand and love ourselves better by caring about and trying to help others in their troubles and distresses. Yes, it may be uncomfortable at times; but those people and situations will act as a mirror for us.

It is far easier to be friendly and supportive of people when they are happy and doing well. We may often shy away from a person once we hear he has a trouble or difficulty. Perhaps we think that we are not adequate to be of any real help. Perhaps we think that that person is probably trying to think of something other than the difficulty, so why bring it up.

And yet perhaps all that person needs is for us to reach out with a caring word or action. The difficulty may or may not become a topic of discussion. What matters is that we took the risk—we risked widening our circle a little bit and we risked discovering something about ourselves by helping someone through a troublesome time.

Experiment: In your efforts to be sympathetic and supportive of others—"to meet our fellow men in their own condition"—try to widen your circle of responsibility. What kind of person or problem do you avoid? Reach out and be supportive beyond the limit of what your habit or tendency would be. As a byproduct, what did you learn about yourself from having done this?

"A smile raised hope; that hope made possible activity; that activity made a haven for some discouraged, disheartened soul.
"Let us smile though the heavens fall, though we may become as naught in a world of selfishness, we may rejoice in the light of Him who has given Himself for our redemption." p. 29

It is remarkable to see how proud the parents of a newborn baby are to see that child smile. It is as if the smile confirms the soul that is now there in that tiny body. There is something uniquely human and spiritual in a smile.

A smile may also be the most basic of nonverbal communications. It has the power to convey a sense of hope. Oftentimes a smile says, "I can see beyond the apparent conditions around us—I can really see *you.*" When we find ourselves centered, at peace and in touch with that kind of hopefulness, let us take responsibility to share it, even through this nonverbal mode. In the words of one Cayce reading:

Do not try to assist self, but rather smile upon those that are downhearted and sad; lift the load from those that find theirs too heavy to bear, in gentleness, in kindness, in long-suffering, in patience, in mercy, in brotherly love. And as ye show forth these to thy fellow man, the ways and the gates of glory open before thee. **272-8**

And what about those times when we do not feel happy or centered? The consciousness of hope and joy is not destroyed;

42

rather it is hidden or blocked. A fundamental principle of changing consciousness says that often "awareness *follows* action." In other words, if we will sometimes act *as if* we had the consciousness (having faith that in fact it is resident within us), then the awareness will actually be able to come forth. Smiling can be such an action to draw forth hope and joy on days when we've lost touch with them.

Experiment: Make it a discipline *to smile* frequently, communicating to others your sense of hope and joy about life. If there are times when you don't feel like it, try smiling occasionally and see if the consciousness follows the action.

Chapter Four
DESIRE

"Desire originates in the will." p. 33

"Erase all desire and you will attain bliss." This philosophy, advocated by some teachers of the spiritual path, sounds simple and straightforward, even though not easily attainable. However, we might wonder if it is really desire that stands in our way. Our human experience suggests that nothing great is accomplished without a strong desire to see it done, so why should this not pertain as well to the spiritual path? In fact it is quite likely that desire, properly directed, is one of the necessary ingredients for us to fulfill our spiritual purpose in the earth.

Perhaps too often when we consider desire, we think of it in terms of a selfish application. But we should begin looking deeper into its psychological and spiritual roots. Desire originates from the sense of incompleteness. Something deep within us feels that it is not yet whole. This is true because, until our conscious selves find oneness with God, we are in a state of separateness or fragmentation. There is the great impulse that drives humanity—the desire to be complete.

The impulse is directed by the individual's will, the capacity to choose. But how is the will able to act out this impulse? It is through the creative instrument we call mind (not just intellectual mind, but the intuitive, imaginative, feeling components of mind, also).

Desire is at the heart of our capacity to change any condition—to move closer to wholeness with God or, by misinterpreting the impulse, to move further apart. In the following two brief passages, Edgar Cayce points out how crucial desire is for the healing of any difficulty:

There will first have to be the arousing in the mental forces

in the body, [2997], the *desire* to get better; the *wanting*—deep down in itself—to get better. . .   2997-1

Q-16. Could Carrie Everett. . .be healed through me? and in what way?

A-16. By gaining first that sincere desire on the part *of* Carrie Everett *to* be, *want* to *be,* healed! Then there may be raised within self that that will overcome those destructive forces that are *eating* at the vitals of the physical body.

Q-17. In what way?

A-17. By first—there *must* be the *desire,* that can only come within self.

Q-18. I have four ways of healing. Which shall I use?

A-18. There must first be the *desire* on the part *of* Carrie Everett to be healed! You cannot create them, no matter what thou hast! *God* cannot save man that would *not* be saved!

281-3

The readings go on to distinguish between a wish and a desire. Like some desires, a wish is a response of the mental body to a physical condition. The difference, however, is that a wish is not an ingrained or repeated response. We might expect that a wish is often directed toward something new or novel in our environment (e.g., wishing to visit a vacation spot you have just read about; wishing you had a car like the one you saw yesterday).

In the Cayce readings desires are separated into three categories. But remember that they are linked by a common sense of incompleteness. When we have mistakenly believed that something in the material world can—*of itself*—remove the sense of incompleteness, then we tend to build desires of the physical body. For example, if I repeatedly turn to food as a way of temporarily relieving psychological and spiritual components of separateness, then I build habitual desire patterns into my physical body. If I mistakenly assume that certain mental ways of seeing and thinking about myself can—*of themselves*—remove the sense of incompleteness, then I build desire patterns into the mental level. For example, if I believe that seeing myself as a famous person or a powerful person will by itself make me whole, then I may create a habitual desire pattern for experiences of this nature.

Finally, there are desires in which I might realize that God is the only thing which can relieve this sense of incompleteness. It does not mean that I stop dealing with the physical and mental world; but it does mean that I remember their limitations. Working with a spiritual ideal regularly is what keeps us oriented toward this third way in which desire can influence us. It is by using the will to call frequently to remembrance what we have set as a spiritual ideal. The way in which we use the will helps us to select one of these three ways to apply the fundamental impulse called desire.

Experiment: Be aware of how you are using your will and observe that by your choices you are strengthening certain desires. Try to make choices that will reinforce those desires which lead you closer to your ideal.

Example: Choose to take an evening walk rather than have dessert, etc.

"The positions in which we find ourselves are drawn to us through our desires. Whatever we are physically, mentally or spiritually has been built through desire." p. 33

We are already familiar with the principle that mind is the builder and that our current life circumstances are the result of what we have mentally created in the past. However, we may add to this the following principle: ". . .*desire* is that impulse which makes for the activity of the mental body. . ." (276-7) It follows that our present life circumstances are largely produced by the *quality of our desires* in the past.

Desire is so potent a force in shaping our lives that the parameters and dimensions which are defined by our desires become a type of personal *law* which our soul will experience. For example, suppose an individual was extremely desirous of personal power over others. That desire could become the law under which he would experience in the future. In other words, every potential experience would be viewed from the perspective of how it might lead to more personal power.

This does not mean that a law created by a desire pattern supercedes universal laws. It is instead like this analogy. Driving on a highway, a woman sees a sign that announces a 55 mph traffic law. Because she desires to travel safely and desires not to get a ticket, she allows her experience to be governed by that law. This does not, however, refute the mechanical law that says her car is built to be able to travel 85

46

mph or the physical law which says that sound or light can travel at speeds far beyond 55 mph.

In the following reading Edgar Cayce refers to how such a law could be created in an interpersonal relationship through desire. A married couple asked about the likelihood of future incarnations together.

Q-9. Is it probable that we will again be closely associated or separated?
A-9. This depends upon the desire. For as creative activities are applied, what ye desire becomes law.   5265-1

Now, how can we take this principle—that desire builds and creates our future conditions—and apply it in a way that engenders hope? Undoubtedly we all have desires of a spiritual nature which are in keeping with our ideal. They may be to see peace and understanding in the world, they may be to see fruits for some service project, or they may be to experience God's presence. Whatever it is, how can we find hope and assurance that those desires will someday be fulfilled?

There are probably times when we doubt or feel that the fulfillment may only come by chance. Yet right before us there are pieces of evidence that should assure us and bring hopefulness. Try this simple exercise. Select something manifesting in your life now which you count as a blessing (e.g., a relationship, a home, a child, a job, your health, etc.). Then examine it and see if you can discover how it came into being as a fulfillment of desires you had in the past. Then use this as evidence, as proof, that the promise will be fulfilled. Those desires we now hold highest *will* in their time come into manifestation.

Experiment: Be aware each day of how past desire patterns have created or led you to specific conditions which you count as blessings. Use this remembrance as an aid to keep a hopeful attitude toward the future fulfillment of spiritual desires you now hold.

"Our mental desires that are to laud ourselves, to appraise ourselves above our fellow man, make it possible for carnal desires to become stumbling blocks in our experiences." p. 34

Recently some psychologists who specialize in motivational

theory have suggested that most of human behvior is influenced by a desire to feel significant or important. In fact each of us *is* important; each one is a unique and infinite creation. Why, then, do we suspect that such motives of self-importance get in the way of spiritual growth? It is simply because things are not at all the way they seem to be.

Perhaps it is because the person who loudly proclaims his own self-worth usually has quite the opposite thing going on deep inside himself; the person who is intent on proving or asserting his own self-worth invariably has a *poor* self-image. It's *not you* he is trying to convince of his worth, it is himself. For example, the person who is pushy and grabs for authority may not be one who has a strong sense of mission to lead. He may instead be a person who has no faith in his own capacity to be directed inwardly, no faith in his ability to resist outside leadership and authority should it violate his own ideals or desires. In such a state of self-doubt (even unconscious) such a person may grab for authority lest he discover himself to be a weak follower of someone else.

In fact it takes a person of high self-regard to be truly humble. Humility is not the same thing as fearfulness or timidity. Humility comes from strength. It is not self-abasement, but instead a simultaneous glorification of God, others and self *in their oneness.*

But how can we move to this kind of inner strength and humility? What if we realize that we have been doing things out of a desire to make self seem important? The key to humility is the recognition of the goodness and equality of all souls. If we have not yet fully discovered our own goodness (which might have led us to greater humility), perhaps we can start with affirming it in others. And what we see in others must be in ourselves as well, particularly the good things we see. As a discipline, then, let this be our desire: to recognize and affirm our equality with all others.

Experiment: Replace desires to appear better than others. Try to hold in mind a deeper desire of the soul to know its *equality* with all other souls. Try to say something good about another.

"Let us pray, 'Lord, use us; let that which Thou seest is best be done in and through us at this time.' Let that mind be in us that

was in Him, who asked nothing for Himself, but went about doing good." p. 35

This passage from *A Search for God* affirms a desire to let God unfold our lives in accordance with His plan. It asks that we might do today the good which we can and trust that what is needed at this time will be given. The passage is therefore also a philosophy of *dealing with the future.* It suggests that we build the best possible future for ourselves by doing the best we can right now.

As much as we all might like to live in the now, we find our desires directing us toward thoughts and daydreams of the future. What are the effects of these desire patterns concerning the future? Do they increase the likelihood of the events happening or do they act as a hindrance? The answer may lie in how we use those desires. If the focus of our attention is upon the *form* or the *appearance* of that which we desire, then they may act as a hindrance. Probably we all have a tendency to allow desires to pre-form the future. We may think out in detail exactly how we want things to be and these pre-formed thought images may block us from responding to events as they really are when that time comes.

For example, imagine a young man who makes a dinner date with a young woman for a week in the future. In the intervening days he may spend hours thinking about what he desires to have happen: what she will say and do, how he will respond. When the day of the date arrives and they are at dinner, it is as if there are *three* people present—the man, the woman, and the man's thought images built by desires of what she would be like. Since he has tried to pre-form the future, he may find himself *performing* at dinner, nervously saying lines he had rehearsed in his head for days. In fact he may spend the entire evening interacting with the third party and rarely interact with the actual woman at all. (Lest we be concerned what the woman will do all evening, we can imagine that she has these same pre-forming tendencies and likely is interacting with the *fourth* party present.)

However, there is an alternative to "pre-forming" as we deal with our desires about the future; that is, to focus on the *spirit of what we desire.* In other words, what did the young man really want? It was a harmonious evening with his friend. He tried to predetermine what actions or events would be required for that feeling and that spirit to be present, and he was painfully wrong. If he had spent the preceding week thinking of the coming date in terms of his desire for there to be harmony between the two of them, things might have been different. If he had *sensitized* himself for a week to *look for harmony,* he might have been able to enter the evening without hindrances and blinders. He might have been sensitive to each moment and the opportunities which were offered to him for the creation of harmony.

Experiment: When you find yourself desiring something for the future, refocus that desire away from "pre-forming" *how* it will happen. Instead focus attention on the *spirit* of what you desire to have happen. When the time arrives for these future events, try to be in the now and to be creative.

"In making our physical desires one with the will of the Father, we will pass through conditions in our experience similar to those of Jesus, who became the Christ." p. 35

Once again we can look at the life and teachings of Jesus for an example of how to work with one of the steps in our *A Search for God* growth sequence. It seems clear that His example is to *give* to others. Both in the way He lived His own life and at the heart of His teachings, this central theme of giving is found. How then, we might ask, does the process of giving provide a solution to dealing with our desires? If we are not yet able to give as fully as Jesus did, how can we *adapt* His example to our development and still remain true to the process and spirit of what He did?

The fulfillment of desire involves something coming to us which we do not already seem to have. We must say "seem to have" because in many cases the thing that would fulfill the desire is within ourselves. We do not realize it is there; or, even if we realize it is there, we are not sure what allows it to come forth. If the law says "to receive you must first give," *what* are we to give in order to receive that which will fulfill our desires?

Perhaps we can best view the perplexity of this question by considering an example. Suppose that a man had a skin condition which created an unsightly appearance. He would no doubt desire a healing of that condition. If the law says that he must give to others that which he wishes to receive, what is he to do? He cannot tell others what to do in order to heal their skin conditions because he does not even know how to handle his.

One solution lies in looking deeper into what the man really desires. What he desires is a change in consciousness, a new awareness about his body and a new self-image. We might ask him, "If your condition were healed, how would that make you feel, what would be the change in your experience of life?" He might answer that he would feel more secure in social gatherings and he would have a sense of being more at peace with himself. It is in this answer that he finds a solution to what it is he must give. He must try to bring into the lives of others a greater feeling of security in social gatherings. Perhaps that will mean seeking out shy people at parties and bringing them into the activities. He must try to help others find greater peace with themselves. Perhaps this will mean making special efforts to be a good listener to friends who are burdened by a problem.

Now, what happens as the man does these things? The skin condition does not necessarily go away automatically. However, what he has done *in consciousness* is to develop around himself a vibration of people feeling more secure in social settings and more at peace with themselves. *One or both* of the following things will happen. He will find himself becoming at peace and secure even though the physical condition may or may not change. Or he will attract to himself knowledge and circumstances that will lead to an actual physical healing. We could depict in chart form this man's experience. It shows him trying to apply the principle of giving for the fulfillment of a desire.

Conscious Desire	Experience or Feeling if Desire Fulfilled	How to Bring Those Feelings to Others
skin condition healed	more secure in social settings	involve shy people in activities
	at peace with self	good listener to troubled friend

Experiment: Work with the principle of giving to others in order to fulfill a specific desire which you select. Create a chart similar to the example above, using the personal desire you have chosen. Try to apply the items you list in the third column.

"...It was a great comfort to me to know that the Master had a similar choice to make, and that in love He overcame desires of *the flesh. My prayer was, I cannot bear this alone, my Savior, my Christ, I seek Thy aid." p. 36*

We are likely to discover that in dealing with some of our desire patterns, we need a source of help which seems to come from beyond our personal, conscious selves. Whether this source of help is from the God within or another soul, it is experientially perceived as an intervening and reconciling influence. Let us consider how often we stand in need of such help in working with those desire patterns which seem to have become a hindrance to our growth.

Many people find that they get caught in an ugly sort of polarity in wrestling with a desire. On the one hand they have periods in which they seem to have broken the control which the desire had over them. This can be accompanied by a type of self-complacent sense of accomplishment at having tamed a part of oneself. But unfortunately this kind of will power usually can only hold the desire pattern in abeyance and out of sight for a brief time. When it returns, it is often stronger.

Then people find that they swing to the other end of the polarity, being controlled once again by the desire pattern and feeling great guilt. That guilt will often manifest as anger or crankiness or depression. But what we discover is that this cycle of temporary taming followed by guilt will probably never get us where we want to be.

The frustrations usually inherent in fighting a desire at its own level hold true for physical desires (e.g., eating, sex, food, etc.) as well as mental desires (e.g., finding fault with others, having power or fame, etc.). In these cases we are, of course, talking about desire patterns which are not in accord with our spiritual ideal and which we would like to change.

What we need is an intervening and reconciling influence which can *introduce a new perspective* on the difficulty. What we need is a new consciousness about the whole matter. As long as we stay in the taming/guilt polarity, we are asking the wrong question. That is why we have not found a lasting answer. What must come first is an openness to receive help, without a bias as to how that aid will come to us and appear. For example, we should *not* say, "Yes, I'll accept help on healing this desire pattern, but only if it comes as a voice from God in meditation."

If we can achieve this sense of openness, then there are two things we can do to help it come. The first is to answer clearly the question: What is it which I really desire? Is the apparent desire a mask for something deeper? Do I criticize others because I really want them to like me but fear they think they are better than I am? Do I smoke because I want to be free from my nervousness and anxiety?

The second is to link the overcoming of the desire pattern's control to some reason beyond just yourself. Is there a benefit that would come to others if you moved beyond this habitual control? Is there good you intend to do for others with the energy or time which, until now, the desire pattern has drained?

With answers to these kinds of questions clearly in mind, all that is left for us to do is to affirm regularly (in words or just feelings) our openness to receive assistance. It is an assistance that does not necessarily make the problem go away but introduces new dimensions, new knowledge and a new framework.

Experiment: Select a desire pattern for which you alternate between taming it and feeling guilty for allowing it to control you. Try to get clear on what it is you really desire. Is the apparent desire only a mask for a deeper desire? Try to see clearly how a change in this habitual desire pattern could also benefit others. In order to keep a sense of openness to receive help, use this affirmation or write another version of it in your own words: "I cannot bear this alone, my Savior, my Christ, I seek Thy aid."

"If we desire to know whether we have chosen wisely, we should ask ourselves, 'What is the desire that is being gratified by the attributes of the relationships being sought?'" p. 37

One of the most interesting things to observe about human relations is the variety of ways that our different relationships can make us feel about ourselves. Take a moment and consider half a dozen different relationships. Don't you notice that when you are interacting with one of these people your self-image and your outlook on life is in some measure different than when you are with a different person? It can be amazing to consider the wide variety of selves within each of us and the capacity of different friends, associates and acquaintances to draw them out.

This realization can be a useful tool for us in considering how we selectively allow certain desire patterns to shape our lives. This is because to some degree the people we choose to spend time with reflect our desire patterns. Since we know (even unconsciously) how certain people bring out certain parts of ourselves, our choices in human interactions may reflect what parts of ourselves we desire to be experiencing. Of course, in considering our interaction with other people, we may claim that we currently have little choice in whether or not we see particular people each day. For example, family members and work associates may be people you will surely encounter tomorrow, unless you choose to lock yourself in your room all day.

However, most all of us have some free time and choice of companions for certain periods. Many can choose whom to have lunch with, whom to socialize with, even whom to call on the telephone for a chat. It is especially in how we use this discretionary time—whom we invite to share our free time with us—that we get a good clue as to what desire patterns most directly influence us. In completing this kind of self-analysis, remember to ask yourself how a particular person's company makes you *experience yourself.*

Experiment: Spend free time or discretionary time with people who awaken in you a self-image or an outlook on life which you think you most need now in your growth.

Our Father who art in heaven,
  Hallowed be thy name.
Thy kingdom come. Thy will be done;
  as in heaven, so in earth.
Give us for tomorrow the needs
  of the body.
Forget those trespasses as we forgive
  those that have trespassed and do trespass against us.
Be Thou the guide in the time of
  trouble, turmoil and temptation.
Lead us in paths of righteousness
  for Thy name's sake.   p. 39

The Lord's Prayer—offered here in Edgar Cayce's version of how the Master gave it—might be considered an especially good affirmation of spiritual desire. Much of this chapter has focused on ways of dealing with the type of desire which can be a hindrance to spiritual growth. But let us recall that there is also a level of desire which not only comes from the depths of the soul but to which it is necessary for us to progress in the evolution of consciousness.

Let us also recall the essence of desire—the impulse to be complete, to be whole. If we can regularly keep this perspective of desire in mind, if we can continually realize that the desire to be whole and complete is good and God-given, then we may be able to adopt a new framework and consciousness toward other desires. Those desires which temporarily give the body, intellect or emotions a feeling of being fulfilled are not wrong or bad. They are available to us as shadow-like reminders of a more profound completeness that will be ours. It is when we stop short that we err. So much of human confusion in the earth is due, not to entering into an experience, but in failing to carry it out fully enough in consciousness to see its meaning. We stop at the point of fulfilling lesser, personal desires without going on to see that they are the shadows of something far greater.

This prayer, then, can be a continual aid to us. Particularly as we use the Lord's Prayer in such a way that it has the highest personal meaning, it can reorient us to a perspective of desire— spiritual desire for completion—which influences our every human experience.

Experiment: Rewrite the Lord's Prayer in your own words, just as this Cayce reading gives its own version. First try to get in touch with your deepest desire to be attuned to God, then let this personal desire be expressed in the way you work each line of the prayer. Try using your version just before your meditation period.

Chapter Five

DESTINY OF THE MIND

"Truth may be proved only by results. If we would be led by the Spirit that leads into all truth, we may expect to have many opportunities for proof in our own life. We alone can judge as to that which is truth for ourselves." p. 43

What is truth? Pilate's question could have provided one of Jesus' most important responses, but Pilate did not wait for an answer. This perplexing problem—at the heart of philosophy—affects us all in everyday events, not just in our profound periods of wondering and searching. Many times every day we want to know the truth of a matter; we want a source of direction which we can trust as reliable and truthful. We want our clocks and watches to be accurate and to give the true time. We want our friends and family members to be straightforward and honest, to give us a truthful picture of what is going on inside of them. We want our national leaders to be honest.

However, we may wonder whether or not the truth is the same for everyone. Just how relative is the truth? Are there absolute truths beyond relative truths, ones which can be applied in every person's life? There is phenomenology, a study of human experience found in philosophy and psychology which accepts as relative truth the experience of the individual as he or she perceives it. In the past 20 years experimental psychology has also become much more sensitive to the way in which the experimenter or observer actually affects the experiment or event he is trying to measure "objectively." That is to say, in his search for pure, objective, unbiased truth he must be aware of the subjective quality of his measurements.

Even the Cayce readings make reference to the personal and individualized criteria for what constitutes truth. In readings about psychic ability he points out that what is evidence for one person to confirm the validity of ESP will not be evidence for someone else.

All these suggestions of the relativity of truth and evidence may be rather disheartening if we are faced with a problem and need to know what is right to do. We might like to know the absolute truth about the matter, not a relative truth which we suspect is colored by biases from our own subconscious. A person will often voice the dilemma in this way, "How do I know whether or not my 'seeming guidance' is really true and coming from God or whether it is just out of my own subconscious mind?"

However, to be able to answer that question, another one must be answered first. What is the criterion for truth which you have previously been feeding your unconscious, inner self? In other words, by your daily thoughts, statements and actions you have defined a particular level of tolerance for deviation from the truth. Virtually all of us have some degree of deviation but the amount differs. For example, if I promise to myself that I am going to give up sugar, how true to that statement am I in the following days? If I break my intention and, in a sense, lie to myself, then what have I fed to my unconscious? What is my definition of the amount of tolerance I allow for deviation from truth? If I tell someone I will meet him at 10:00 A.M. but do not show up until 10:15 A.M., what am I subtly feeding to my unconscious?

We define for ourselves just how absolute and attuned to Divine Truth will be our inner guidance. And it is *not* a matter of the inner self getting revenge for any previous deceitfulness or falsehood we may have committed. Biased or twisted inner guidance is not a punishment from the inner self; it is simply the inner self's operating under the laws and criteria we have set forth.

What is the solution, then? How do we come to know a truth which is beyond the subconscious mind? It is by setting strict standards of truthfulness in waking life. If you say you are going to do something, then do it. If you say you believe something, then act like it. As your tolerance for deviation from truth diminishes in the way you act in your waking life, your capacity to intuitively receive higher truth is enhanced.

Experiment: Be truthful to yourself and others. Let your actions reflect more closely what you have thought, said or intended for your life.

"Destiny is a law, an immutable law, as lasting as that which brought all into being. It is expressed in all the varied spheres of manifestation. We see its signs here and there. . ." p. 43

These next three chapters of the *A Search for God* growth sequence focus on the concept of destiny. In order to relate to what that can mean at the physical, mental and spiritual levels, we should consider just what the word "destiny" implies.

First it suggests something about the future. Most of us are curious about the future. We wonder to what degree things are already set in motion to turn out a certain way. To the extent that we feel that our future is rather predetermined, we may turn to possible signs or indicators to get a clue as to what is just ahead. This may mean astrology, numerology or a wide variety of similar studies.

However, these indications reflect our *past*. An astrological configuration is best understood as a picture of where the soul is coming from. Those who study Cayce's astrological references in life readings will notice that most of those readings limit astrological references to planetary sojourns (i.e., experiences at nonmaterial dimensions of consciousness) between earthly lives.

Nevertheless, for some people these signposts of the past are helpful in looking ahead. This is because destiny has almost as much to do with our past as it does our future. But it is far more than just the fact that our future actions are predictable based on the habit patterns we have built in the past. Admittedly, if I have a habit of taking a particular route to the office each morning it is very likely that my future holds in store more trips along that very route. But the issue of destiny is much deeper than that.

Destiny is just as concerned with our past as with our future because of what occurred in the *far distant* past—our creation. An inner course was charted for each soul and, even though free will was made available to deviate from that course, there would always remain some impetus, some force or influence within the psyche seeking to get back on that course. There is within each of us a gyroscopic activity—an impulse to fulfill that for which we were created.

And so, our destiny is not just a goal that awaits us in the future. A static notion of destiny misses the whole point. Merely a standard to which we are obliged to measure up some day fails to include the dynamic quality of destiny. Even without our conscious effort there is an impetus toward that goal. There is a continual influence and impulse of that inner gyroscope to keep us on the track of expanding awareness. That influence brings us inner urges and promptings *and* it brings us into situations and encounters which are perfectly matched to what is needed. A first step for us in moving more efficiently toward our destiny is to trust the dynamic, active quality of destiny.

Experiment: Nurture a sense of trust in life. Allow events to come to you rather than trying to force things to happen the way you think they should. Trust that inner, directive influence of your soul's destiny that will continually bring to you things to keep you on the best course.

" 'Love one another'? Yes, the whole law is fulfilled in love, in 'Thou shalt love thy neighbor as thyself.' " p. 44

What do you know of loving? How has life taught you about love? For some people the answer to this question is a very beautiful love relationship, perhaps a romance or the love between a parent and child. It is in such circumstances that we most easily discover our own capacity to give to another and to care.

However, as Jesus has pointed out, just how challenging is that? Does not almost everyone love a person who loves him back? How deeply does that require us to reach inside ourselves and explore the depths of what love means? How much do you really know about loving if you love only those who love you?

Probably we have all asked ourselves that question. And probably each of us has felt a kind of determination to do better. We sense that we are built to be loving creations and intuit that we can love more than just the person who has love to give back. And so, in our enthusiasm to try harder, where do we begin? Perhaps with that most difficult relationship where there is a lack of cooperation or even animosity. We are determined to love this person despite all the obnoxious things he or she does.

Nevertheless, what do we often end up doing? Suppressing resentment? Or perhaps behaving more politely to the person directly but behind his back or in our thoughts still being critical or unforgiving? If you have observed any tendencies like this in your own efforts, perhaps another course of action is called for.

The approach just described is like a person who looks in the mirror one day and says, "I've got to lose twenty pounds!" So he goes on an ambitious workout program and overdoes it the first week. Discouraged by the pulled muscles or exhaustion, he gives up. What he lacked was an optimal growth sequence. He was inclined to tackle the hardest kinds of exercise first and his burst of initial enthusiasm and determination undermined his efforts.

Learning how to love is very similar. We need to develop the psychological and spiritual muscles for loving. To take on your most difficult relationship first may not be the place to begin. Instead you must look for a progressive curriculum of challenges. A better beginning point for most of us is a third and little considered category of people in our lives. In one category are people who are already actively loving us and, in the second, those who are actively sending back to us things contrary to love. But what about the third category—people we rarely notice—those who are not giving anything back, love or unlove?

Love those who have no love right now to give back. This is a perfect starting point for many of us to explore more fully our capacity to care and serve. It may be a very withdrawn person. It may be a child, an elderly person or even someone who is sick. Because we have not been receiving energy from such people— positive or negative—we too easily forget them. But it is in developing these kinds of relationships that we learn some of our most important lessons about loving.

Experiment: Notice people around you who seemingly have no love to give right now: those who are neither actively loving you nor actively directing ill will at you. Find ways to love people in this category of your life.

"And we know that all things work together for good to them that love God. . ." p. 44

This Biblical principle is not intended to hold out hope that we can make a deal with God: I'll believe in You and You make everything go smoothly in my life. Instead what it promises is that those who love and follow the teachings of the Lord will find an integrative, harmonizing influence in their lives. Things will "work together" and not at cross-purposes. Each event, no matter how troublesome in appearance at first, will be part of a bigger picture of something good unfolding. In the words of one Edgar Cayce reading:

He who doubts that the best will come to him with doing of that which is correct is already defeated. Don't blame others for what has happened or may happen. Do right yourself, physically, mentally and spiritually, and the best will come to you.   **5203-1**

If this promise sounds attractive, how do we put it into action for ourselves? One might say, "Yes, I love God but how do I get a better sense of things working together?" Two types of mental discipline may help with this need. First is an exercise in looking back. When something manifests in our lives that we experience as a blessing, we can take time to review how it came into being. What past experiences led you to be right where you *are* now in order to be able to receive that blessing? Were any of those events the kind that caused you to doubt while they were happening? Sometimes in regularly looking back to see how things have worked together to create good in the long run, we can develop strength and insight to see the same process in progress with our current challenges.

A second exercise is to try to meet life events with *optimism*. We can bring to our various circumstances those feelings of hope and an openness to receive what comes. In doing so, we will often feel things working together for good even before that good is physically manifest. A particularly effective place to practice this discipline is in situations where there is an interruption to the flow of what we intended to do or get done. What is our response? To view the interruption as a nuisance, as a detour to what needs to be happening?

Consider the following example. No doubt you have had a similar experience. Before leaving for work one morning, a woman has her regular quiet time for meditation. She meditates on an affirmation concerning a desire to serve others. Ending her meditation, she looks at her clock and discovers she is running late. Driving to work, she is in a hurry. At this point we see that she has a strong flow of intentions (i.e., to make up for lost time and be at work on schedule). However, she keeps hitting red lights and her progress is slow.

As she finally gets within about two miles of her office, she sees one of her fellow employees standing helplessly by the roadside, discouraged at apparently just having missed the last public bus to the office. Of course, the driver pulls over to the side of the road and gives the fellow employee a lift to work. Had she not been delayed by those red lights, she wouldn't have had the right timing to help this man.

This story is admittedly a simplification of the process because often we do not see quite so quickly how things are working together to allow us to fulfill the ideals we have set and meditated upon. And in this story we have not said what the woman's reaction was to hitting all those red lights. Was she frustrated? Or had her meditation put her in a place where, despite the desire to be at work on time, she was willing to accept with optimism any event that might otherwise have seemed to be a nuisance or detour?

Experiment: Meet circumstances which interrupt the flow of your intentions with optimism and a belief that you can make the interruption part of a process working together for good.

"Not by thought do we change this or that, but by constant thinking, constant building." *p. 45*

From time to time we hear the principle, "What you constantly think, you become." And no doubt that scares many of us into more constructive thought patterns, at least for several days. Most of us would not want to become some of the thought patterns which we entertain even occasionally.

As a pioneer in the field of holistic health care, Edgar Cayce was very aware of the way in which consistent positive thinking was a key ingredient in the healing process. To one person who had a condition of paralysis, he directed these words:

Yet we find that with consistent and persistent application these may be materially aided. However, it will require persistence and consistent activity; not only in the material applications, but in the attitude and the relationship of the mental self to Creative Forces or God.   1705-1

We might wonder what it is about our thinking that allows thought patterns to actually be built into the physical structure of who we are. What is the connecting link? Apparently it is not just the constancy of the thought but the *emotionality* of it that is the decisive factor. In other words, if we will examine our habitual, repeated thought patterns we will discover for most all of them an emotion is attached.

For example, if I keep thinking about my dentist appointment next month, perhaps there is an emotion of worry attached. If I keep reliving in my imagination an argument with someone, there may be the emotion of resentment, anger or even self-pity. But whatever the emotion may be, *it* is primarily the thing that links thought to what I become. The endocrine gland system of the body reacts to the emotional component of a thought and chemically expresses that emotion to every cell of the body via hormones placed in the bloodstream. Lest we feel discouraged by all this and the examples of negative emotions, let us recall that emotions of joy, happiness, love and hope can also be expressed by the endocrine system, and we can just as easily build these emotions in our physical structure.

Looking more closely at the emotion attached to a constant thought pattern, we discover a second important fact. Often the emotion itself is what we have grown attached to and *it* is producing the continual thought pattern. For example, it may be that I am somehow attached to the emotional resentment that followed an argument. It is not so much that I want to think about the events over and over again. Instead, it is that I have no sense of resolution to my resentment and the constant thinking pattern is the *product* of this emotional statement.

To change constant thought patterns which might make us into something we do not want to be, we must work with the origin and not the byproduct. The origin is usually the emotional pattern we have not resolved, replaced or ceased enjoying.

Experiment: At the end of the day, just as you are going to bed, take several minutes to review your thoughts of the day. What recurrent thought patterns do you observe? What is the emotional component related to each one? For those you would like to change, do one of three things:

1) Select a potential replacement emotion to hold the next day.
2) Try to resolve the emotion by thinking about it or praying about it.
3) Make a commitment to let go of the emotion if you see it is merely a negative one you have been enjoying.

"Christ came into the world to teach us how to think constructively, in order that we might return to our original estate. 'Let this mind be in you, which was also in Christ Jesus, Who. . .thought it not robbery to be equal with God.' " p. 45

One way of stating our destiny is that we are to be conformed to the image or the pattern shown to us by Jesus. Jesus' life is particularly of interest to us in our examination of the mind's destiny because in the Trinity the Christ corresponds to the mind (with the Father corresponding to the body and the Holy Spirit to the soul).

What do we know from the Biblical accounts of Jesus and His teachings to give us an insight to the destiny of our own minds? The passage quoted above, from Philippians 2:5-6, is perhaps the most succinct statement which we have. It suggests that it is the destiny of our minds to claim our divine nature. It suggests that our minds must come to that point of being able to affirm that we are gods.

But why is this so hard for many of us to accept and to say to ourselves? Why is there that tendency to deny our own divinity and point to all our shortcomings as proof that we could not be gods? And how different is that kind of denial from the one Peter made three times just before the Crucifixion?

Of course, our affirmation of divinity must be tempered with something. In writing his letter to the church at Philippi, Paul not only encouraged us to have a mind that would affirm equality with God, but also went on to say that Jesus also humbled Himself and became a servant, that He was obedient, even to the fulfillment of the purpose for His life. We must accept the whole package. To use another Biblical phrase, we must "put on the whole armor," not just the part that seems most attractive.

Here, then, seems to be a significant aspect of our growth toward fulfilling the mind's destiny. It starts with an affirmation of who we know ourselves to be. Yes, we may have clothed ourselves in non-godly attire with thoughts, desires and feelings. However, what is beneath that attire is unchanged. Just as the reluctant prince who was hesitant to be king tried to run away from his identity and escape his responsibility, we may be inclined to deny our divinity. But the story, full of archetypal imagery, concludes that the prince cannot escape his heritage—nor can we.

Experiment: Use as an affirmation for the day (not for meditation but in waking life events) "I am a god." Be sensitive to the creative potential and the responsibility which this entails.

"What would we have our mind-body become? Let us remember, it becomes that upon which it feeds. . ." p. 45

Do we ever think of feeding the mind the way we feed our bodies several times daily? Even though we may not be very conscious of it, we do feed the mind continually. Its diet is made up of what we read, what we watch on television, the kind of music we listen to, the types of conversation we engage in.

Perhaps we can take some of the principles of a physical diet for attunement and apply them to a mental diet. That is, if the process is the same—taking in particular vibratory qualities of energy—then the laws which govern the feeding process should be applicable at whatever level we are observing. In studying the mental level of feeding, let us consider three aspects of the law regarding good physical nutrition:

1. Certain things in and of themselves are toxic to a body and should be avoided. For example, in a physical diet we might want to avoid refined white sugar all the time. What are things you might have been feeding your mind that are probably unhelpful all the time (e.g., a particular television show, a particular kind of reading material)?

2. Certain things are to be avoided in combination with other things. For example, Edgar Cayce says do not drink orange juice and have a whole grain cereal at the same time. It is a matter of the context *and* the *timing*. What are things in your mental feeding patterns that need to be avoided in certain contexts or at certain times (e.g., not to listen to a certain kind of music just before going to bed, not watching a particular type of television program while eating)?

3. A balanced diet involving a variety of foods is necessary. No one food will have all the nutrients which are needed. How balanced and varied is your mental diet? Do you spend all your free time for reading on just one kind of book? Do you have friends who only want to talk about one kind of topic? Consider if there is anything you need to change in order to have better variety and balance.

Experiment: Work with applying the three dietary laws described above in the way you feed your mind.

"Hence, as our thoughts, purposes, aims and desires are set in motion by mind, their effects are as a condition that IS. In dreams we attune our minds to those storehouses of experience that we have set in motion." p. 48

One of the most exciting features of dream study is precognition. The Cayce readings and many other sources have pointed out evidence that the unconscious mind has the capability to look ahead and see what may be in store for us. This ability to see the future should not be understood as a future which is fixed. It is rather a matter of probabilities and likelihoods. The precognitive dream is saying, "If things continue on the pathway they are now on, here is what is likely to happen."

It is analogous to being on a journey by foot along an uncharted trail. One might climb a tree from time to time in order to be able to see farther ahead. From this other point of view one may or may not decide to continue in the direction currently being followed. Similarly a precognitive dream may lead us to the decision to change our course of action.

Frequently the role of dreams in decision-making is misunderstood. While it may be true that occasionally we will have a dream which clearly shows us exactly what decision to make, nevertheless the majority of our dreams, even precognitive ones, do not make the choice. Instead, the dream provides us with a perspective of what the mind (through thoughts and desires) has set in motion. Why do we need such information? Simply because most of the time we do not realize what we are doing. We are relatively asleep to the implications and consequences of the way we use our minds in daily living.

So, a precognitive dream is not necessarily a message from God. To have dreamed something and later seen it happen as dreamed, does not *necessarily* mean it was planned by God or willed by God. Too often people will say, "My dream told me to do such and such." Instead they should usually say, "My dream has shown me what I am creating for myself in the future."

The fulfillment of our destiny is enhanced by working with precognitive dreams in conjunction with a spiritual ideal. Only with this second factor can one ask, "Is the likely future event which my dream suggests I've created for myself actually consistent with the path I want to follow?"

Experiment: For a week take special note of your dreams and note the precognitive process that is in many dreams. You will find dreams that predict the physical manifestation of things which you have set in motion at a mental level. If these dreams of physical events do not look favorable to you, work on changing your thought patterns. Observe whether or not such a change in your thinking immediately affects your dreams.

Chapter Six
DESTINY OF THE BODY

"Jesus used the words, 'abundant life,' abundant experiences, to show the extent of God's goodness to His children that they might come to an understanding of their oneness with Him." p. 53

The message throughout the Bible is that the Lord is a God of abundance. "The earth is the Lord's, and the fullness thereof." (Psalm 24:1) There need not be a condition of lack on this planet—for food, for energy, for love or anything else. Simply by reading the story of the miracle in which Jesus fed the five thousand, we must be touched by the power and the will of God to provide plenty. Recall that not only was the group fed, but there was an excess which was collected.

What is it that characterizes abundance? What images does that elicit in our minds? Probably of conditions in which there is *more than enough*. Perhaps this image provides us with one key in understanding what a God of abundance requires of us. For when there is more than enough available, what are we to do with the excess? We never have to face this problem when things come out even, when supply exactly fits demand. The challenge comes when conditions are out of equilibrium (i.e., when there is not enough or too much).

When supply is *less* than demand, then we are forced to select priorities, to decide on basic values, to determine our ideals explicitly or implicitly. When you run short of cash, you have to make some basic decisions about what is most necessary or important to have. When a nation runs short of food, leadership has to decide who is going to get enough to survive.

However, when supply *exceeds* demand, you are faced with the problem of what to do with what is left over. We may smile to ourselves and say, "Oh, that's a problem I wish I had more often," but how well have we handled it in the past?

Several fundamental courses are available to us. One is to waste or throw away what is left over. Not too many years ago our Western world had so much petroleum-based energy available to us cheaply that in many instances we wasted it. Individuals waste talents; many people waste or kill their leisure time. But to waste any resource—collective or personal—is to invite the slow withdrawal of its availability.

A second course of action is to hoard the excess in fear that there will not be enough later. The ancient Israelites did this in the wilderness, but the manna they stored away from the abundance ended up spoiling. A lack of faith in God's future abundance may end up isolating us from it *and* at the same time undermining the resources we have hoarded out of fear. That is not to say that we should lack prudence. Preparation both collectively and individually for the possibility of future needs may be required. But does that preparation come from faith and inner direction (e.g., Joseph's interpretation of Pharoah's dream in Genesis 41) or does it come from fear and doubt?

A third available course of action is to go to great lengths to try to insure that there will not be an excess. A law of business management warns that work will expand to occupy the amount of time allotted to that activity. Consider how this would operate in the following hypothetical situation: Mr. Barker has been given a project to complete by his boss Mrs. Edwards. Although he could have completed the project in four days if he worked at his potential peak efficiency, he was told he had five days to get it done. Sure enough, he found enough things to do so that it took all five days. In other words, a clear possibility existed for an abundance—more than was needed. But a way was found to avoid having to deal with problems that might have been created by time on his hands and no project on which to work. Perhaps another example of this course of action is found in American grain policy. There are, no doubt, strong arguments demonstrating the economic advisability of the practice, but it seems ironic that in a starving world our government pays farmers not to produce as abundant a crop as they easily could.

A fourth course of action available is to deal responsibly with our excess. Responsible actions will look different in different circumstances. There is no easy formula and the food and grain situation is a good example of the problem. However, perhaps the *answers* to *huge* problems like world hunger, energy shortages, etc., can come only after enough *individuals* begin dealing responsibly with their own *little* situations. There may be little you can do quickly to change hunger or poverty on a mass scale on the other side of the planet. However, each of us can begin to bring into the vibrations of this earth a new consciousness. It is a new sense of creative response to the challenge God offers a *few* of us through abundance.

If you do not have an abundance of dollars, look more closely to see another point where abundance touches your life. Do you sometimes have an abundance of free time? Of a talent or skill? Perhaps we begin to change the greater world conditions by how we act responsibly with our personal abundance.

Experiment: Practice bringing greater *abundance* into your life and the lives of others. Give of your excess—your time, your money, your talents, your energy—in some area that seems to need it without any thought of what you might "get" in return.

"It is through the mind that the destiny of the body is gradually builded." p. 53

As we explore the three levels of destiny, we will discover that they are profoundly related to each other. In this passage there is the suggestion that in fulfilling the destiny of the mind, we work to build the destiny of the body. If the body's destiny is an enlightened, resurrected physical vehicle for the expression of spirit, what role does the mind have to play in the transformation which is required?

To answer this, we might examine the capabilities of mind to create and transform energy. One which is of particular interest is the capacity of mind to create an image. We think of our bodies as images, for example, saying, "I looked at my image in the mirror." And, in fact, they are hardened or manifest thought images. In other words, the image which is created when one mentally visualizes the new car he desires is not unlike the image which one sees upon looking in a mirror. The difference is largely a matter of duration, clarity and intensity.

We might consider how the very act of visualization can potentially play a significant and helpful role in realizing the destiny of the body. There has been considerable confusion in the minds of some concerning what Cayce had to say about visualization; however, upon careful study we see that the principles for and against visualization are quite straightforward. Let us begin with one example when visualization was recommended but with a qualification at the end.

Q-1. Am I visualizing and concentrating on the correct goal for me to attempt to reach and am I doing it properly?
A-1. The visualizing of any desire as may be held by an individual *will* come to pass, with the individual *acting* in the manner as the desire is held. The manners in which this entity is going about the visualizations are well. We would not alter them save in that these be not forced upon anyone that has not had some vision of his own—see?   311-6

The caution here seems to be against visualizing something for someone else. That is, I can use visualization as a constructive tool when it concerns something about myself for which I am responsible. In that category we would find the condition of our own bodies and the quality of our own responses of attitudes and emotions. For example, I might visualize healing moving through each section of my body. Or I might visualize myself replacing a resentment toward someone with a feeling of forgiveness and cooperation. However, as a general rule, it is best not to use visualization for someone else's body or to see someone else thinking or feeling differently. It can also become a misuse of visualization in many cases to imagine particular material possessions one wants. It may "work," yes. But can we really evaluate if that possession was what we needed right then?

To use visualization as an aid to fulfill the destiny of your body—that is, health and perfect integration with mind and spirit—try using regularly a mental procedure similar to the steps described below.

(1) Get into a comfortable position, sitting or lying down.
(2) Focus your attention for about a minute on your slow, deep breathing.
(3) Take a total of at least two minutes to move mentally through areas of your body, beginning with your feet and moving up to the ankles, calves, etc., on up to your head. At each point, feel the life and energy of that part of your body, the consciousness which is there. Speak to that part of your body, to those cells, and direct them to be relaxed and attuned to the Christ Consciousness.

(4) Now work with visualization and awareness at the level of each of the seven spiritual centers. Move from the first center (the gonad center) up to the seventh center (pituitary center). Spend about a half a minute with each one. Apply that Edgar Cayce reading which says to fill each center with the ideal. You may wish to visualize the white light at each of these points. Most importantly feel a sense of your spiritual ideal touching and healing the patterns of energy stored at the respective centers.

(5) Close the exercise by feeling your body to be a channel of light and take a few moments to pray for others for whom you have concern.

Experiment: Complete the exercise in visualization for your body described above. Try it regularly for several days.

"...we should understand that sacrifice does not necessarily mean a giving up, rather it is the glorifying of the body for a definite purpose, for an ideal, for a love." p. 55

Like the word "obedience" with which we worked earlier, "sacrifice" is a misunderstood and unpopular term. In a society of high standards of living and material progress, the idea of doing without something does not sit well. However, we might wonder whether this difficulty is created out of mankind's rebelliousness and selfishness *or* out of a misunderstanding of what the word means.

Most people confuse sacrifice with another word which begins with the same letter: surrender. In other words, for them, to sacrifice something means only one thing—to give it up. But we would arrive at a better understanding of sacrifice if we were to begin with the spiritual level and to consider what happens in our *consciousness* when we truly make a sacrifice.

If I am asked to sacrifice something (rather than asked to surrender something), then what is required of me is to change the nature of my relationship to it, to redefine the place it has in my life. This may necessitate cutting energy ties to that object or person, in the sense of no longer allowing habitual response patterns and thinking patterns to control me. However, it does not necessarily mean that that object or person leaves my life.

Admittedly the way we use sacrifice is usually to remove the person or object from our lives. But this is a drastic measure and actually a shortcut which is easier to do. For example, if someone felt compelled to sacrifice sex, the actual call is to redefine what role sex plays in that person's life, to change the nature of his or her relationship to it. This would mean letting go of old habit patterns of thought, feeling and action and establishing new ones. The easiest thing a person might do would be to remove that whole level of human experience from his or her life. But the deeper challenge would be to continue that level of experience with a new consciousness toward it—that is, to glorify it "for a definite purpose, for an ideal, for a love."

Historically, how was sacrifice performed? In a symbolic way, our ancient ancestors would kill an animal, which represented mankind's own lower nature. For example, the archetypal symbol of the gonads is the calf or bull, and the ritual killing of such an animal demonstrated our ancestors' misunderstanding of the whole process, a tendency which has carried over into today.

Recall what Jesus said of sacrifice. God does not wish a killing but instead mercy. In other words, killing off aspects of our physical nature is not the answer. What we seek is a resurrected, enlightened body and that is achieved by redefining our relationship to the drives and desires of the physical body. If uncontrolled urges to eat certain foods stands between us and God, then indeed a sacrifice is required. But it is not in the sense of surrendering all food. Sacrifice is in lifting the act of eating into a new consciousness. It is in glorifying eating by seeing it in terms of an ideal and a love of the body instead of an unconscious and habitual act.

Experiment: Sacrifice something related to your body—not in the sense of giving something up, but rather to lift that something to a greater sense of purpose or love.

"We have each been given stewardship over a portion of life (God)." p. 55

We are caretakers of great resources provided by God. Among these resources we may count our intelligence, talents, ideas, money, possessions and even physical health. In many of Jesus' teachings there seems to be a strong emphasis upon the right attitude and the right use of resources over which God has made us stewards.

Perhaps the best remembered example of this is the parable in which one man buries the money entrusted to him, fearful that it might be lost. Another man takes his own share and puts it to use. In the end the man who was fearful and did not use that which he was given was chastised. Our *first principle* of stewardship could be summarized in this way: "It is our responsibility to apply in the world the resources over which God has given us stewardship."

In a second passage from Jesus' teachings, He suggests that if we are faithful and use well the small amount of resources we have been given, then we may be able to receive and be responsible for more. And furthermore, He seems to say in the passage below that in order to receive spiritual resources we must demonstrate our responsibility with physical resources (i.e., mammon) given to us by God.

> He who is faithful in a very little is faithful also in much; and he who is dishonest in a very little is dishonest also in much. If then you have not been faithful in the unrighteous mammon, who will entrust to you the true riches? And if you have not been faithful in that which is another's, who will give you that which is your own?
> *Luke 16:10-12*

Our *second principle* of stewardship, then, states: "To receive a greater amount of physical resources or to receive higher, spiritual resources, we must first be faithful with our stewardship of what we now have at hand."

Finally, there seems to be increasing responsibility of stewardship as the amount of resources under one's control becomes greater. Jesus' way of saying this states succinctly our *third principle:* "Everyone to whom much is given, of him will much be required." (Luke 12:48) And part of what is required of us is to see that worldly goods are distributed and dispensed in a way which reflects the equality of mankind. One Cayce reading in particular refers to this ideal of good stewardship for those who have been entrusted with much:

> It would be well for the entity, then, to turn again *within!* For, know, as He hath given, "The silver and the gold are mine, and the cattle on a thousand hills." Hence those who put their trust in righteousness and judgment (not of men, but of the purposes that self may be the channel *through which* there

74

may come aid and help and understanding and awakening) may become those channels through which the worldly goods may be dispensed and disposed of in ways and manners to the glorifications of those purposes and causes *within!*   877-5

Experiment: Make a list of those things for which God seems to have given you stewardship or care. Attempt to behave in specific ways which would demonstrate a more careful, responsible sense of stewardship. How could you better invest, put to use or nurture these things? Try working with a consciousness of the three principles of stewardship just described.

"It is with right thinking and right acting that we keep the holy temple pure. He stands at the door and knocks. It is necessary to keep our temple clean. . ." p. 55

The process of "keeping our temple clean" involves both the mind and the body. However, for purposes of this chapter on the destiny of the body, let us focus on procedures for purifying the body through physical means.

First, we may wonder why it is necessary to purify ourselves in order to know God. Is it some sort of divine reward system which requires us to measure up to some standard of cleanliness before God will notice us or give us what we want? This kind of thinking may have been ingrained from childhood when our parents would say things like, "You are not going to be allowed to eat until you have washed those hands." Now, of course, there may have been good reasons for our parents to have made this or similar statements; but, if this notion of "get clean to get rewarded" carries over to our adult concept of God, then we probably misunderstand the law.

Instead, it is for our own protection that we do not have access to higher, spiritual energies and consciousnesses until we have cleansed ourselves. This is because whatever is within us will be magnified as these higher energies move through us. It would not be to our long-term benefit to have impurities magnified, even though we might like the temporary "high" of a premature spiritual experience.

How do we go about cleansing the body? As we have already noted, there is a mental component because the very chemistry of the body is affected by our thoughts. We can become toxic largely through attitudes and emotions. However, for this experiment let us focus on additional, physical procedures for cleansing the body. Here are four areas on which to work:

1. Eliminate toxic foods. Certain foods cause a stress on nearly every body (refined sugars, white flour, etc.). Other foods are more individualized. You probably know of some foods to which you have an allergic reaction or which merely make it harder for your body to function optimally. Remember the word "optimally." Do not try to get by on saying just, "Oh, I still get along okay when I eat that." The question is, instead, "What food allows your body to operate *best?*"

2. Cleanse the body internally with water. The Edgar Cayce readings recommend 6-8 glasses of water daily. Most nutritionists suggest that this drinking of water be between meals, so as not to dilute digestive enzymes.

3. Exercise. Not only can physical exercise directly aid elimination through the skin and bowels, but it can also help to move toxins out of tissues (where they have been stored), enabling their removal by one of the body's elimination systems.

4. Enhance eliminations. Try a colonic (if they are available in your area), a castor oil pack or a steam bath. All of these help the body in its natural channels of cleansing itself.

Experiment: Work on purifying your body for one week through diet, exercise, cleansing or whatever ways you can.

"All things are possible with God. Do not expect results in a day; for we do not sow one day and reap the next, but we reap what we have sown in periods when that which is sown comes to fruitage." p. 56

Nearly every spiritual teacher has said that we must learn to live in the now. Jesus said this quite explicitly in "Therefore do not be anxious about tomorrow, for tomorrow will be anxious for itself." (Matt. 6:34) And yet for almost all of us, this is a difficult thing to do. Especially in a world which seems to be going by so quickly, which is so filled with things which have to be done, it appears that if we do not continually keep one eye out for what is coming next, then we will not survive.

This tendency to hurry from the present moment to a future

moment is so characteristic of these times. Many people reach the painful point at which they continually want the present moment and event to be over so that they can get on to the next one. Unfortunately, when they do get on to the next one, it is met with the same restless attitude. Take a look at your own life and see if there are recent instances in which you were living that way.

What is behind this tendency to hurry? No doubt there are slightly different reasons for each person, but perhaps there are underlying similarities. We may have become too goal oriented, too concerned for seeing the product of what we are doing. There is a measure of impatience in us when we fail to see results quickly. But this means that we have forgotten the importance of the *process* of getting something done. There can be joy and fulfillment not just in seeing an accomplished and finished product, but also in the act of creating it and allowing it to come into being.

Another underlying similarity in our tendency to hurry is the belief that there is not enough time. If I am impatient for what is happening now to be over, it may be due to a sense of pressure I have created for myself. I may have subtly fallen into the belief that God and life will not allow me enough time to get done all that I feel I must do.

These misconceptions and confusions do much to create a feeling of dissatisfaction and unfulfillment for many people. In contrast to them are principles which we will try to experience and apply in this experiment. First is that God's timing is the best timing. There will be time for you to get done what really needs to be done and the opportunity will be there at the best time. Make the best use of this day and what is happening right now. Learn to enjoy even the process of something which is slowly being accomplished.

Experiment: Live with a sense of contentment with the now. Let go of any feelings of being rushed or wanting the current moment to end so that you can get to the next thing.

"Hence, with what body shall we be raised? The same body we had from the beginning! or the same body that has been thine throughout the ages! else how could it be individual? The physical, *the dust, dissolves; yes. But when it is condensed again, what is it? The* same *body. It does not beget a different body!" p. 57*

How can we speak of a destiny of *the* body when we have before us a succession of lives each with a different body? What good does it do to work on purifying the body when we will just have to start all over again later? It makes sense to work on the mind and soul—to actively pursue the fulfillment of their respective destinies. However, this is because they are nonmaterial and not subject to decay.

This kind of reasoning is fundamentally in error, according to the Cayce readings. A key to understanding the destiny of the physical body is in the very definition of physical which the readings employ. The physical domain is a range of vibration, a particular dimension. Specifically we think of three-dimensional experience as physical. Yet things can have a three-dimensional expression and still not be seen: for example, infrared light or X-rays. The physical body can be thought of as a multifaceted creation, which includes not only a flesh manifestation but an unseen body of higher vibration (yet still "physical") which Edgar Cayce called the "finer physical body." In this case "finer" does not mean "better" but rather "of a more rarified or higher vibratory quality."

The finer physical body can be thought of as continuing on after death. In the next incarnation a corresponding manifestation in the flesh will be condensed. But in the most profound sense, it is, as the quotation above states, "the same body that has been thine throughout the ages!"

An analogy might be helpful here. Recall the simplest way to observe the existence of a magnetic field. In school you may have seen this demonstration. Place a magnet under a piece of paper and scatter iron filings on top of the paper. The filings create a picture of the unseen yet very real physical force field around that magnet.

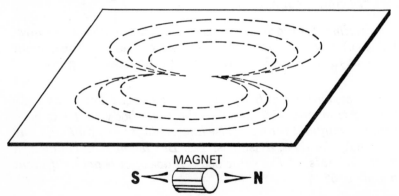

MAGNET
S ◁ ▭ ▷ N

In this analogy the magnet is like the finer physical body, and the pattern assumed by the iron filings is like the manifestation of a flesh body. At death the magnet is removed and the filings free-scatter and lose the pattern's identity. However, the magnet could be taken to another piece of paper and once again recreate a pattern amongst a new set of filings.

This very principle immediately raises some questions and problems. Why wouldn't I look the same incarnation after incarnation? How could a soul change sex from one incarnation to the next? Does this mean that we can judge a person with a deformed body to be currently expressing the *sum total* of what he has built into his finer physical body for ages?

The answer to these problems lies in an addition to the theory. It says that not all of the physical potentials of the finer physical body are necessarily manifest in the flesh at one time. For example, we might expect that the finer body is not essentially of one sex or the other but has the potential in a given incarnation to manifest one or the other. Similarly, a deformed flesh body does not represent the entirety of what has been physically built by that soul. And what, we might wonder, determines the aspects of the finer physical body which will manifest in the flesh? The mental patterns and the purposes of the soul for that incarnation.

This addition to our theory requires us to qualify the magnet analogy. Like most all analogies, there is a point at which they break down and do not depict fully all that one wants to say. In this case there are two major shortcomings. First, it fails to illustrate that the flesh body is only one aspect of all the potential patterns stored within the finer physical body. Second—and very crucial—it fails to show that the changes and work which we do on the flesh body alter the finer physical body as well.

This second point is so critical because it provides a way for us to sense that we are in fact working on the destiny of our bodies. It gives us a link to something which is ongoing and not bound by time and mortality. Dr. Herbert Puryear, one of the most insightful interpreters of the Edgar Cayce readings, has pointed this out in the following recommendation: If you have been rubbing peanut oil into your arthritic knee joint for months, but knew that you were going to die tonight in your sleep from some other ailment, it is still worthwhile to rub that oil in again just before going to bed. The beneficial effects you have on that finer physical body will carry on over.

Experiment: Treat your body in a way which reflects an awareness that it is eternal.

"Let the light of His countenance guide us. He, our Lord, is willing, if we use our body, our mind, our abilities, as channels of expression for Him." p. 58

In what ways do we make our bodies channels of blessings for God's expression? Certainly through varied acts of service; but perhaps nothing better exemplifies this ideal than the way we use our bodies in meditation. In meditation there can be the experience of attuning or aligning the mind and body to what the spirit would have us do.

Too often many of us approach meditation as merely a spiritual exercise or perhaps as a procedure involving just the mind and spirit. However, to experience fully what meditation can mean, the body must play a key role. In fact, it may well be that for many of us to learn to be effective meditators, the important skill we must learn is *how to coordinate physical presence and movement with mental awareness.*

Let us consider a common problem and mistake that many of us have with meditation. It is the direct result of not establishing a mental-physical harmony during the meditation period. We may say our affirmation many times, trying hard to stay focused on its spiritual meaning. We are continually interrupted by mental wanderings or by physical disturbances (e.g., restlessness, uncomfortableness, etc.).

This is essentially one of the two fundamental problems described by the Chinese meditation text called *The Secret of the Golden Flower.* It is to have a high spiritual ideal ("light") without letting go and allowing it to be received harmoniously into the body ("circulation"). What is missing are two items. One is the experience of *surrender*—of letting go, even of our mental thoughts of a high ideal—and *trusting that that ideal will keep on doing its work.* The other missing item is a harmonized mind-body system ready to receive the expression of that ideal.

Here, then, is a training exercise for meditation with which you may work. You may wish to adapt it to suit your own needs but try working with its essential features.

1. Complete your normal meditation preparation (e.g., head and neck exercises, prayers of protection, or whatever you like).

2. Repeat one or more times the Lord's Prayer. Say it slowly and feel its attuning influence on the body.

3. Repeat your affirmation several times. Work with the affirmation until you really have a sense of sincerely being at-one with its spirit. Spend at least a minute or perhaps several minutes on this.

4. Surrender the affirmation. Trust that its influence will not leave you just because you stop thinking about it for awhile.

5. Turn your awareness and attention now to harmonizing mental awareness with physical presence. For approximately 50 breaths let your awareness be as totally as possible upon *just* the flowing in and flowing out of each breath. Count silently if you wish, but do not be in a hurry for the breath you are currently on to be over. You need not think about your affirmation. You have already in step 3 sincerely invited that spiritual ideal to express itself. Trust that it will respond in its own way. It doesn't need any more coaxing nor can you make anything happen. Merely let your mental awareness be fully on this most primary of all physical processes: breathing.

6. Close with another period like step 3 or, if you prefer, go directly to your period of prayer for others.

To illustrate this exercise in diagrams, there are three stages. In the first stage we are already very aware of the body and mind, so they are represented in capital letters. The spirit is only dimly perceptible, so it is represented in small letters. First, the mind focuses on the spiritual ideal (through the tool of an affirmation). In the second stage, our feeling of this spiritual ideal is now magnified by this focus of awareness. However, as long as the mind hangs on or tries to make something happen, it blocks things from happening in meditation. In the words of

BODY   MIND ——————→ spirit

Stage 1

BODY   MIND ——————→ SPIRIT

Stage 2

BODY ←————←——→ MIND   SPIRIT

Stage 3

The Secret of the Golden Flower we have "light without circulation." In the third stage, the mind and body harmonize. For example, we might do the awareness-of-breathing exercise. This provides a *receptive medium* for the spirit to express itself in whatever way is most needed that day.

Experiment: Practice using this training exercise for meditation. Let it carry over as well into your daily living. In tense times take a moment to think of a spiritual affirmation, then harmonize mental awareness with breathing. This can be done with your eyes open, even in the midst of daily affairs.

Chapter Seven
DESTINY OF THE SOUL

"Through the will, however, we may make those things that are of dishonor as stepping-stones to positions of honor." p. 63

Once again we come back to a principle found repeatedly in the *A Search for God* readings and in many other descriptions of personal spiritual growth: making stumbling blocks into stepping-stones. However, in this case the text asks us to look at a particular kind of potential stumbling block. It is the type of experience which we feel has dishonored us.

The notions of honor and dishonor may seem a bit anachronistic, more readily identified with historical periods hundreds of years ago. Some people would say that in our times right and wrong, good and bad, have been so relativized that it is difficult to judge when one's honor has been violated. But this is a view of honor in terms of whether or not *someone else* has infringed upon our *own honor*.

Instead of using this approach, the *A Search for God* material suggests that we view honor as an internal process. The question changes from "Did that person's behavior dishonor me?" to "Did my own behavior dishonor myself?" It becomes a matter of identifying those experiences in which we did not live up to the best we knew to be doing.

Most likely we all have experiences from the past which we feel dishonor the best that is within us. These may be actions that we are ashamed of having done or for which we criticize ourselves when they are remembered. And for many people such memories are frequently recalled. Considerable energy is expended by many people in guilt and condemnation for what they have done that in the present seem to dishonor themselves.

The question then faces us: how to turn such stumbling blocks in spiritual growth into genuine steps forward. The way *not* to do it seems quite clear. Guilt and self-criticism accomplish little or nothing. Instead the answers may lie in the *lesson* which was to be learned by the experience, dishonorable as the experience may have been. If we can *let go of dwelling on those past events* and start living more directly the lesson which was learned, then the experience has become a stepping-stone.

Perhaps a simple example will best illustrate the process. Suppose a man is scheduled to give a brief talk at his community group. Rather than prepare, he is confident that he can do it off the top of his head. But when the time comes he rambles through the talk, getting confused and generally doing a poor job. For weeks afterward he thinks back to that experience, ashamed and embarrassed by how poorly he did. However, this "dishonor" can be made into a stepping-stone if he will turn his attention away from a continual replaying in his mind of the unfortunate events. What was the lesson learned? It was the necessity *for him* to plan ahead more and to prepare. As he looks to the present and future to apply that lesson—instead of feeling guilty or criticizing himself—the dishonor becomes a stepping-stone.

Experiment: Select an experience which might be called a dishonor for you. It is likely to be something you find yourself being ashamed of, embarrassed about or criticizing yourself for. Turn around your response to this. What was the lesson you learned from what happened? Try to put that lesson into action in your life rather than continually dwelling on those past events.

"Opportunities are presented to us through physical experiences for using and directing the soul powers lent to us by God. The way we use these powers in relation with others shows the concept or degree of awareness of our attunement with God." p. 64

Each of us is here in the earth with *unique* abilities and talents to fulfill a purpose. We might think of them as "soul powers." Even the person who does not think that he or she has any particular powers, in fact does have the special potential to get something done better than anyone else could. Certainly it may not be anything impressive which that person is here in the earth to do—at least not impressive from a material point of view. However, it is the destiny of each soul to discover just what those unique powers may be and then to put them into application.

There is a simple way to start that discovery process. It begins by asking oneself, "What are the things in which I have faith and confidence to do well?" It may be commonplace actions, such as cooking or repairing a car. It may be a special sensitivity to interacting with others, such as raising a child or being a counselor to friends. A crucial step in fulfilling our destiny lies in identifying just what it is we do well and then *building on those strengths.*

So often and so easily the spiritual path is viewed as a wrestling match with oneself. But the path is walked in the most optimum fashion by building upon what we do well rather than fighting against what we do poorly. Being balanced and whole does not necessarily mean the ability to perform every aspect of human experience with great skill. A great artist does not necessarily have to become a master logician in order to be whole and fulfill his soul's destiny. By identifying what he does well—his God-given "soul powers"—and using them in service to humanity his destiny is accomplished.

The same holds true for each of us. What are the things which you know you do well? Make a list of them. Then for each one consider how you could build on that particular strength. No matter how insignificant or commonplace, it is a type of soul power. Building on that strength means using it in such a way that more people benefit from it.

Experiment: Make a list of what you have faith and confidence in to do well. Select one item and identify what "soul power" might be associated with it. Use that power more often or more effectively to help others.

Example: "I am good at home repairs." The soul power—the God-given talent—might be a mind which is insightful about how physical things operate or good eye-and-hand coordination. Now how could you be doing an even better job of using what has been given to you?

". . .if we consider that slights, slurs, and unkind words are directed against us, and we remain untouched within and can rise above the selfish desire to strike back, then we can

understand what Jesus taught as he urged us to seek attunement with the Father." p. 64

An especially difficult challenge presented to us by life is how to respond to actions or events designed to harm us. The variety of choices is often confusing, made all the more so because historically so-called spiritual people have demonstrated reactions ranging from pacifism to "holy war."

It is a classic problem which seems to defy a simple solution. Probably we have all faced the situation many times. Because we want to grow spiritually and demonstrate love for others, we determine to be nice to those we contact. Then someone does something to us which is blatantly meant to discredit or harm us. Someone steals something from us, speaks rudely, lies to us or whatever. Inside of us there is a classic argument which may sound something like this: "If I do nothing but just ignore the offensive behavior, then I only encourage the person to do it to me again. If I react with a harsh word or aggression, I may deter the person from treating me like that again, but I will feel guilty for acting that way."

The dilemma does not appear to present a ready solution. Merely turning the other cheek seems to invite things to continue the way they are going. Striking back promises at best a temporary cessation of the offensive behavior but may produce hard feelings. At worst the assertive or aggressive reaction could escalate the problem.

Perhaps what we should remember is that Jesus said more than just "turn the other cheek." He taught that we should love and do good to those who hate us. In other words there are *three* alternatives: (1) do nothing, be passive, let it roll off your back; (2) fight back, "an eye for an eye"; (3) do something which may well startle the other person—be loving in return.

To fulfill our spiritual destiny it is not enough just to practice the first alternative. In fact it will often fail to bring any healing to the situation. Perhaps it is only in the third alternative that there is found the necessary shock or stimulus to move that person's consciousness to a new level so that the offensive behavior can be ended.

Experiment: Respond to slights, slurs or any offensive behavior of others directed at you with words and deeds reflecting love.

"Each time we resent, we add to these confusing urges that become stumbling blocks for us." p. 64

Resentment can be one of the most paralyzing influences to our efforts to grow into a higher consciousness. It saps the mind of creativity as it demands a mental replaying of previous occurrences. It keeps us locked in the past instead of looking to the present and the future. Learning to forgive and let go rather than holding on to a resentment is a skill in consciousness which is indispensable to the fulfillment of our spiritual destiny.

How is this skill developed which allows us to forgive instead of resent? One pathway is to first examine the anatomy of a resentment. What is it that goes on within us to produce this common human experience? The key to our understanding of resentment lies in seeing how profoundly our own self-image affects our personal psychological make-up.

As a general rule of thumb, we should remember this principle: "How I feel about myself deeply affects how I will feel about you." Applying the principle to an understanding of resentment, it would suggest that if I resent something which you said or did, it is because of something related to how I see myself. However, it must be a matter of something more specific than merely words or deeds which are offensive to the image I hold of myself. For example, suppose a person said something to me such as, "The work you did in the office yesterday was lousy." I might not like to hear these words, but let us suppose I was able to take them in, evaluate for myself whether or not they were true and then let it go. There might be no resentment, no continual replaying of the event later in my mind and no hurt feelings.

However, suppose that later that day someone saw me out dancing and off-handedly commented that I looked awkward and silly. This might produce a resentful response on my part. For days or weeks I might find it hard to get over my anger or hurt feelings for this person having made that comment.

The question then remains as to why one event produced a resentment and the other did not. The answer may lie in my own self-image. Imagine that I have a strong self-image of myself at work. I do not think I am infallible but nevertheless I have had enough positive experiences and positive feedback at work that I feel a certain sureness of myself in this area of life.

However, I do not yet have a strong self-image of myself as a dancer. I dance only occasionally at social events and my self-image here has a certain vulnerability.

A resentment, therefore, may arise as a response from our attitudes and emotions to a threatening behavior on the part of another. A person's words or deeds may call into doubt or into question an *aspect* of self-image we were nursing along *but of which we are not yet sure.*

This insight can provide us with a strategy for dealing with a resentment. Ask yourself, "What image of myself did the person's words or deeds undermine or call into question?" Identify just what that aspect of your self-image is which is not yet fully sure of itself. *Then do things which will help strengthen that self-image.* In the example used previously, I might reach the insight that my self-image as a competent dancer was called into question. To deal with resentment feelings toward that person, the most direct thing I can do is get some more *positive* experiences for my dancer self-image. That might mean some more dance instruction for myself or it might mean teaching someone else a dance step I know so that I will realize that I do have some competency in this area of my life. As this self-image is slowly strengthened, I will find that the resentment dissipates. With my intellect *and* my feelings I will be able to look back at that person's previous words with greater understanding and forgiveness.

Experiment: Select a resentment you have been holding for something which another person said or did to you. What aspect of your self-image was undermined or called into question by what the person did? As a tool to make forgiveness easier and more natural, do some specific thing to strengthen that particular part of your self-image.

"Though there may be periods of trial and temptation, when our purposes seem fraught with disappointments, if our faith has been placed in Him we may find that which will help us grow in understanding and knowledge of His love. . ." p. 66

Anyone who lives life with a sense of expectancy and optimism will, from time to time, probably face disappointments. We can sometimes see how things could work out nicely, but other people or life itself just does not have the same vision of how things ought to be. The person we were in love with does not love us back. The job we had eyes on as the perfect one does not work out. The vacation we had planned for years has to be canceled because of lack of funds. And we feel disappointment.

What does this word mean? The pre-fix *dis* serves as a negation to the root word *appointment*. Looking closely then at this more fundamental word, we might define *appointment* as an agreement between self and another to meet at a specific point in time and in space. There is a quality of intentionality and even purpose to appointments which we make. If one makes an appointment with a dentist, there is a commitment to meet at a certain place, at a certain time for a particular purpose. In making that appointment one has expressed an intention to see that certain things be done (e.g., having one's teeth cleaned and examined).

Dis-appointment, then, means the negation of an intentionality for something specific to happen in time and space. Things do not unfold in the way we had hoped or planned. This often gives rise to discouragement or even depression, but such an emotional response does not necessarily have to accompany the experience of a disappointment. Edgar Cayce points this out to one individual whose disappointments had led to deep discouragement.

. . .because of discouragements and because of failures, and because of heartaches, and because of those things that make men afraid, will ye turn thy back upon the opportunity before thee now?

Then what is the real problem?

Hold fast to that as ye purpose in thy heart—that there *will* be the opportunity for those that are through their own shortcomings losing, or have lost, sight of their relationships.
165-26

If we can remember that there is a profound intentionality within our souls—that there is a destiny of the soul—then we can view a disappointment differently. We can see that when our conscious plans or intentions are denied, it may be due to the fact that God has a different plan for our lives. What we consciously perceive as a "disappointment" is really an indicator that God has an "appointment" for us with some other experience which more closely follows His plan for our lives in the earth.

Experiment: If you find yourself being disappointed in conditions or others, change your attitude by using this affirmation: "For every apparent disappointment, God has an appointment for me with something greater" and look for the *gift* that can come your way with a change of attitude and new receptivity.

"Let us keep an attitude of sincerity, of oneness of purpose; for if we are sincere with self, and most of all, sincere with our fellow man, we will not fear to be called into the presence of our God." p. 66

One Edgar Cayce reading suggests that sincerity is a rare quality in people. This may be part of the reason why so many of us look for it in forming our closest personal relationships. It is as if some deep intuition tells us that the nature of what can happen between us and another individual is largely determined by how sincere we can be with each other.

In another reading Cayce makes what is perhaps an even stronger statement about this quality. It indicates that further development of sincerity may be the primary step in knowing oneself.

Then, the first law of knowing self, of understanding self, is to become more and more sincere with that thou doest in the relationships one to another. For the proof of same is the fruit thereof. And when thou hast found the way, thou showest the way to thy brother. 261-15

How can we define sincerity so as to see why it is so crucial in close relationships and in self-knowledge? The *A Search for God* passage for this experiment suggests the definition "oneness of purpose." In other words, lack of sincerity is found in duplicity, in mixed motives. Lack of sincerity is evident when we say or do one thing but inwardly feel something else.

Therefore, we might expect that self-knowledge is clouded by multiple motives and purposes. Suppose, for example, one is continually acting in a way that indicates one purpose in life, but inwardly thinking and feeling a different purpose. Imagine someone who often acts with generosity, giving of time and money, but inwardly it is with a self-serving purpose, hoping to gain prestige and respect from his gifts. Such mixed motives—

such insincerity—clouds self-knowledge. It is not a matter of the person saying, "Oh yes, I know I'm doing this—I realize I have mixed purposes." That is not the type of self-knowledge the Cayce readings are referring to. Instead, the knowledge which insincerity clouds is the experience of one's own divine spiritual nature and oneness with others. The internal process of mixed motives creates an internal kind of fragmentation or split self. The inward split makes it difficult to recognize the quality of wholeness and oneness which characterizes the deepest sort of self-knowledge.

In relationships we are able to bond ourselves to *only one part* of another person if that person is being insincere. The most satisfying and meaningful of relationships are those in which we feel that we can commit ourselves to the *wholeness and fullness* of who that person is. Others hope for the same from us. Our work may be to examine our purposes and motives. Where we find duplicity there are changes which are required if we want to know our own spiritual nature more fully and if we want to form deeper bonds of love with others.

Experiment: Work on being more *sincere* in your relationship with others, with God, and with yourself. Be clear about your *singleness of purpose* in relationships. Demonstrate more clearly to others just what that purpose is.

"Do we have one standard for self, and another for our friends, for our relations, for those about us? All are one in Him." p. 67

No doubt we have all heard before this principle of evaluating self and others by the same standard. And so why, we might wonder, does it still get us into difficulties in our relationships with others? Why do we still make others resentful or even feel guilty ourselves when we *apparently* use the *same* standard to evaluate our own growth and behavior as we do that of others?

It is too simplistic to say merely "don't judge others." Of course, it is true that we *cannot pass judgment* on another in the sense of that person being ultimately answerable to us. However, we must make evaluations of others in order to function in the world. One has to make decisions about whom to interact with—decisions about marriage, who gets a promotion in the business, whom we will trust, and so forth.

Perhaps the way in which we fall short, the place where we go wrong, is once again to focus too much on form and not enough on process. We need similar *process-oriented standards* in evaluating self and in evaluating others. A simple illustration will make this more clear.

Imagine that you had two children—a girl and a boy who were twins. The girl was very developed intellectually. She was quite good in school subjects like arithmetic and science. The boy was quite developed in terms of his intuitive and artistic side. As a good parent, suppose you decided to use the same standard to evaluate your children.

If your son worked very hard for a month at his math and science and brought those two grades up from D's to B's, how would you evaluate his efforts in comparison with those of his sister who continued easily to get A's? Or suppose your daughter worked for weeks on a clay sculpture, which was far better than she had ever done before but still was not nearly as beautiful in appearance as the one your son could do in an hour. Do you evaluate based on appearance and form? No, it would be done on effort and growth, that is, a *process-oriented* standard.

The same holds true in our daily life evaluations. If I am skillful at giving lectures and a friend is only beginning to try this, I cannot use the same form-oriented standard to evaluate how well he or she has done. If I must evaluate, then perhaps I should think of something I am newly trying to learn how to do. Or, in another example, if I have no trouble with the habit of overeating, I probably *do* have some *other habit* I too easily give in to. If I must evaluate how well someone else is doing in curbing his or her overeating tendency, I should compare it using a similar process-oriented standard. How well am I doing with that which is difficult for me?

Experiment: Measure and evaluate self, loved ones and problem people in your life with the same process-oriented standards. What are the specific types for which you find yourself being judgmental of others? Even though some may come more easily for you, what are your own areas of challenge and struggle? If you need to evaluate how others are doing in their areas of weakness, make your comparisons based on the same standard of how well you are doing with your own unique areas that need growth.

"*. . .to do good, let us use that which we have in hand; the* *environments and experiences that make for changes that are necessary in our life will present themselves. If the preparation is made, the time and place to use our knowledge will come about. It is the law; it is His love." pp. 67-68*

There is a strong cultural inertia *against* applying the spiritual principle to use what one finds at hand. A basis of high-pressure advertising in the media is to create in the viewer's or listener's mind the notion that we have a need and that something which we do not yet have is required to meet that need.

But rather than blame others for this incessant obstacle, we must be willing to take some of the responsibility for its existence and then move on with our growth in spite of it. Our own impatience to have material goods and our own desire patterns have created a climate in which such media barrages have been able to expand and have influence. It can become a type of vicious circle. Our own initial restlessness and impatience to have more was fertile soil for an advertising strategy in our culture which says in effect, "Don't use what you have, buy something new." This strategy, in turn, tends to influence many people even more strongly in that direction of desire.

At some point we need to get off the circle. We need to realize that current conditions often present the resources needed to fulfill our needs. Certainly we can hope for more and better things. However, they come to and are used by us most optimally if we have first used well that which was previously at hand.

It can be fun and rewarding to try meeting a need first with what is already available rather than immediately to run out to obtain something new. Admittedly there are times when there is no way around the fact that a key ingredient or tool or resource is missing and will have to be obtained. Nevertheless, there will be other instances where our own ingenuity discovers a way of adapting and a way of channeling an old resource into a new application.

As we do this at a material level first—in cooking, with home repairs, etc.—an exciting thing happens. The process carries over into psychological and spiritual areas of life as well. We discover new ways to use talents and resources of our minds and spirits. Learning to do this insures that with each new gift that does come our way we will be more likely to experience it in the fullness and variety of what it offers us.

Experiment: Especially at the material level try using what is already at hand to meet new needs which arise. Use your creativity and ingenuity to discover a greater variety of potential in the resources which you already have.

Chapter Eight
GLORY

"GLORY IS OUR ABILITY TO SERVE, which is an opportunity given to us by God." p. 73

An essential teaching of the New Testament is that greatness is in service to others: "He who would be the greatest among you must be servant to all." (Matt. 20:27) Consistent with this, the *A Search for God* readings approach glory as our capacity to serve.

The concept of service certainly includes the very act of *doing* something for someone else. However, most importantly it is an attitude. We can all think of instances in which we were doing something which aided another, but that assistance was only secondary, only a byproduct. Our deeper motivation was that it increased the likelihood of getting something we wanted from that other person.

Service, therefore, must begin with a mental outlook and, in fact, an entire perspective on life. It is a point of view which includes the self but which does not place the self at the center of everything. Here is a four-point summary of what might be included in such a mental foundation for true acts of service:

1. Have no concern for who gets the credit for acts of helping which are done. There is, instead, a desire that the praise go to God rather than self as the servant. One Edgar Cayce reading said it this way:

In these manners, through the effacing of self, these influences may be wrought in such manners that many, *many* will call them blessed, *many* will give the glory to God; not to them, not to their efforts, but that they make themselves channels through which the glory and the might and the power of the Lord may be made manifest! 688-4

2. Enter into each new situation, not with an attitude of "What can I get from the people or these conditions?" but instead with a questioning, "What can I give to this situation?" There are subtle ways in which our tendency may be to look for what we can get from each new encounter. It is not necessarily money or power or any overt thing. It may be a desire to get approval from others or just recognition.

3. Love and serve those who have no love or service to give back. We have already examined this principle in an earlier experiment. Again, it doesn't take much to do something good *for* another if you know it will result in something equally good *from* that person. The real test of love and service is in relationship to people who have nothing to give back right then.

4. Live for something beyond yourself. This is where the joy of living can be rich and full. This is where our pleasure in being alive is not always against a backdrop of anxiety which says: "How can I protect and keep what I have?" Service—and glory—come naturally and freely as we continually remind ourselves of having a purpose in life which reaches far beyond ourselves.

Experiment: Expand the scope of how you think you can serve in the world. For a week try serving others in a way you do not normally do.

Example: Visit a shut-in neighbor or friend. Spend time with children (perhaps offer to babysit to give parents a night off).

"All are called into service. . ." p. 73

Do you ever find yourself measuring and evaluating your own work against that of others? What have you set as your criteria for doing a good job in being of service? Perhaps too often we use an outwardly oriented standard to measure how well we are doing in fulfilling our capacity to be of service.

All are called to serve, but each in his or her *own unique way.* If I sense that I am called to serve by caring for and being sensitive to children, then I cannot necessarily look to another person to see how often or how effectively he or she is doing this particular kind of service. That person might be very insensitive to children. I must not find an excuse or solace in failure to do what I am here to do by saying to myself, "Well, look at so-and-so; she is very spiritual but does not do a good job with children." In fact, that other person may be called to another form of service.

All are called to serve, each with particular capabilities to glorify God. If we understand this principle, it leads us to two disciplines. First, we should use no other person's actions as a standard to decide if our service is sufficient. Second, learn to appreciate the service of others. Oftentimes we appreciate only two kinds of service: that which directly aids us (e.g., the service of an auto mechanic) and the service which is in the same general field in which we are involved.

The following experiment is designed to expand our scope of awareness. By taking time to be sensitive, we can discover a wider range of actions within the human family which God counts as service. Even if we are not personally helped by such individuals and what they do, we can still take joy in seeing another part of humankind fulfilling its capacity to glorify God.

Experiment: Recognize and respect the unique ways in which people around you are able to serve. Even if you are not directly aided by such service nor are you normally interested in such types of action, notice others in this way. If possible, find ways to reinforce these people with a word of support or appreciation.

"With our minds firmly fixed on our Ideal, who always lost sight of Himself, we may glory in service by using our minds to build within us knowledge and wisdom that will fit us for greater opportunities—not to the glory of self, but to the glory of God." p. 74

In some spiritual teachings the mind is often treated in a derogatory way just as is the body. In an effort to impress upon students the supreme place of spirit, some teachers tend by a sort of "backdoor" method to relegate the conscious, rational mind and its companion, the human body, to a lowly role. The body is depicted as the origin of physical desires and drives which have kept us trapped in materiality. The conscious, rational mind is depicted as devious and self-serving, a constant source of hindrance in our efforts to meditate.

Fortunately there are other teachers who feel that every

aspect of human life has a role and a place for good. In resurrecting His body, Jesus affirmed the importance of finite, physical form. Edgar Cayce said that for years before His Galilean ministry, Jesus traveled extensively to learn and study—that is, to train His conscious, rational mind. Some of His later encounters with the Pharisees are beautiful examples of this level of rational mind and of how it can be attuned to serve the Spirit.

There is, therefore, a place for learning and study. Yes, we must eventually go beyond the rational level of mind. We must learn to intuit knowledge. Spiritual truth, in fact, often does appear as paradox and thoroughly befuddles our rational selves. Nevertheless, there is a place for "using the mind to build within ourselves knowledge and wisdom."

Perhaps this is so because the rational mind and the intuitive, spiritually sensitive mind are not so very different. Instead of a dichotomous split of mind, it may rather be that, when the mind works intuitively, it operates at a higher dimension but uses some of the same processes which are involved in rational thought.

By way of analogy, recall grade-school arithmetic. First you learned addition. You may have felt pretty pleased with yourself, but suppose an older brother or sister came along and burst your bubble by saying, "In order to solve the really hard and important problems, you are going to have to put away addition and learn a whole new process: multiplication." Sure enough, the next year you learned how to multiply numbers. To do so you had to learn new relationships. When you saw "5" and "7" together, you had to resist thinking "12" and instead write "35."

What you may not have realized was that multiplication is not that different from addition; in fact, it is merely a more complex yet shortcut way of doing addition. (Example: 7x5 means 7+7+7+7+7.) Similarly, the intuitive, spiritually sensitive capability of the mind may be a more complex, higher dimensional operation which makes use of some of the same processes employed by rational thought. In other words, study and learning at a conscious level not only have their place but may even aid higher workings of mind. The primary temptation to be overcome involves a tendency on the part of the rational mind to become rigid or assume all-knowing abilities as it becomes more and more educated.

This experiment is an invitation to make some renewed

efforts to work at properly training the logical, thoughtful part of the mind. These efforts may in many ways help you become more capable of serving.

Experiment: Make it a discipline each day for a specified time period (e.g., half an hour) to read or study in some way which opens up a *new* area of knowledge or learning for your conscious, rational mind. Then, see if you can find ways of using the rational mind in what you have studied and learned in *service* to others.

"So may we, for self-glory, for the approval of man, offer to our Lord that which may bring our destruction." p. 74

Pride exists out of harmony with God's system of changing and evolving consciousness. This is because the prideful person has become locked-in to a particular self-image and rigidly holds to it. In such a case there is a continual need for reinforcement by others, for approval which says in effect, "Yes, that really is who you are."

However, in order to grow we must often let go of our pride— we must enter into situations in which we no longer have the approval of others. Imagine that life brings to a person some condition which humbles him. Perhaps the person has been law-abiding and is very proud of it, yet finds himself by an extraordinary set of circumstances in jail one day. Or perhaps it is the student who has always made A's and is very prideful of her ability, yet one day discovers there is a subject of study at which she just cannot do well. The event, in itself, humbles the individuals, destroys their pride, *but also* presents the opportunity for them to develop a new kind of sensitivity and tolerance.

The following illustration depicts how we get pridefully locked-in to a particular image of ourselves. In order to move on and grow in consciousness, life brings us changes which can give the *appearance* of a temporary movement *backward*.

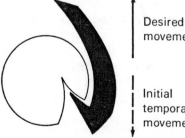

Desired movement

Initial temporary movement

What are we to do with these reversals? What if we have taken great pride in *being an example* of some principle to others? The answer is that we can continue to be an example even when we are humbled and our pride shattered. The prideful, law-abiding citizen can still be an example. In this case, it is not the form of what a perfect citizen looks like, but instead the process of how best to behave and react after one has been stopped for breaking a law. The straight-A student who suddenly finds herself doing poorly in one class can become an example of persistence in learning something which is difficult.

In summary, then, we may expect life to challenge us to change from time to time. Especially we must change when the following conditions have arisen: (1) one is locked-in to a self-image, thinking highly of self and less of others, and (2) one looks for approval from others for this self-image. If we do not act on our own accord to change such a situation, then life itself will at some point humble that prideful side of ourselves. Perhaps it will give us a temporary setback but along with it the opportunity to get back on a growth pathway.

Experiment: Examine an area of your life in which you are facing a reversal, setback or obstacle. Is some part of your self-image being frustrated or even humbled? Might this situation have come to you in order to help you overcome some sort of pride? From this new perspective try meeting the situation with a new consciousness.

"What is evil? It is good misapplied, good used to satisfy the desires of self." p. 75

This is a revolutionary philosophical concept—that good and evil are not poles apart. It is a direct corollary of the principle which says that the One Life Force is not neutral but is essentially good and loving. Yes, with our free wills we can use the One Force in such a way that it brings pain or destruction. But the universe has an impetus toward integration and wholeness. What we call bad is something which had the potential in essence to be good but which was turned around by an individual's free will. Two Cayce readings state it this way:

For what is bad? Good gone wrong, or something else? It is

good *mis*applied, misconstrued, or used in a *selfish* manner—
for the satisfying of a desire within self.   1089-5

How far, then, is ungodliness from godliness? Just under,
that's all!   254-68

As easily as we may be able to agree that this philosophy
sounds appealing, it becomes a difficult challenge to put it into
operation. To see just how hard this can be, consider that for
many people one of the most baffling of Edgar Cayce's
readings says that we must learn to see the *essence* of the
Christ's love even in the vilest of passions. (254-68) It is
certainly much easier and much neater to be able to toss out
despicable forms of human behavior. Many religious teachings
settle for such a shortcut method which draws sharp lines
between opposing and equally strong forces of good and bad.

These principles can be used in the way we view and treat
characteristics within ourselves that we label as bad and those
qualities in others that we criticize or condemn. If Edgar Cayce
is right, then even the most selfish or evil-appearing of
behaviors has behind it a potential to be used in a more loving,
creative way. The bossy, aggressive person may have the
potential for leadership if certain qualities were not misapplied
or misconstrued. The unreliable person who is always late may
have the capacity to flow truly with the moment and be free of
anxiety and worry if he or she can learn to balance with a sense
of personal responsibility.

There are examples of Jesus using this principle. The
capacity of the centurion to recognize authority in a military
sense (and some considered the Roman army to be evil) also
allowed him to be able to recognize the spiritual authority of
Jesus and to have unparalleled faith. Similarly the fiery
personality of Peter was turned from getting his own way to
devoted commitment to fulfilling God's way.

Experiment: What is something seemingly "evil" or "bad" in
the personality or behavior of *one* person with whom you
interact? What is the *essence of good*—good misapplied or
misconstrued—that is in that apparent flaw? Try reinforcing or
reflecting the essential good which is there.

*"Do we want to be guided by His Spirit, to be a portion of that
Word which shall not pass away? If so, then indeed we are right*

101

to respond to the urge from within to 'carry on,' even though everything seems to contradict the practicality of doing so."p. 76

Is there practicality to a spiritual life? In other words, can we measure and evaluate the efficiency of things without slipping into a mere materialistic view of life and ourselves? To answer this question, we must begin with a closer look at what it means to be practical, in the commonplace sense of the word.

Suppose that you owned an oil well in Oklahoma and after months of pumping oil you were now getting only a low-grade oil out of your ground. Imagine that it reached the point where the energy consumed in pumping out one barrel of this lowgrade oil was actually greater than the energy which could be derived from that barrel of oil once it was refined. At that point, it would not be practical to carry on with the pumping at that spot. There would be a net loss in measurable or perceivable energy.

When we translate this analogy to human affairs, the word *perceivable* becomes especially important. It implies that we may be able to expand our consciousness in order to become aware of benefits being derived from our efforts which were not previously noted. For example, suppose that years after closing down your oil well, it is discovered that your particular kind of low-grade oil happens to have traces of some highly valuable mineral. Now you may decide that indeed it is practical to start pumping again.

All this is to say that practicality is a relative matter and that relativity is determined by the scope of one's awareness, knowledge or consciousness. When we face a decision about whether or not it is practical to persist in an endeavor, one of our preliminary questions should be, "Have I considered to the best of my ability *all* potential benefits being derived from my expenditure of time and energy?"

In human relations how are we to evaluate if the efforts we are making are really practical? For example, when you love someone and do not immediately receive love back, is it impractical to persist and carry on? If we narrow our consciousness and look only at physical appearances, we might conclude that, yes, a lot of energy is being put in and not much is coming back out. However, it may be that a spiritually oriented practicality does not judge by appearances. With heightened sensitivities we may be able to perceive changes and effects which balance the equation quite nicely.

Experiment: What is some seemingly unrewarded effort you have been making for good—something you have recently been considering giving up? Try for one week just "carrying on" even though it may go against *common* "practicality" to do so, and see what happens.

"In service, without thought of personal gain, comes that which makes for the greater growth of our soul." p. 76

The growth of the soul is toward the awareness of oneness. The message of this section on Glory is that through selfless service to others our growth toward oneness is achieved. How is it, then, that service to another person allows expansion of consciousness to take place?

The key lies in the following principle: "Our self-definition is determined by that to which we give energy without a sense of duality. If I expect something in return (even if it is not necessarily to come from that source), then I have a duality and not oneness." To expand upon the parenthetical phrase in that principle, imagine that we are helpful to another, not expecting anything back from that person, but still expecting a reward or approval from a third party. In that case we still have a duality, and the apparent "service" is not really service at all nor is it growth toward oneness.

All of this can be illustrated in the following diagrams:

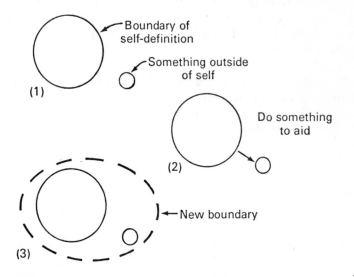

(1) Boundary of self-definition — Something outside of self

(2) Do something to aid

(3) New boundary

I am one with that to which I give energy and love without thought of return. It is the thought of return which creates a sense of duality. However, I can expand the boundary of how I have defined myself. Up until now what has kept that boundary tight and narrow has been demands and expectations on my own part. In other words I have not wanted "to be taken advantage of" by others. I may have been careful to receive back at least as much as I put out. But if I can drop this demand, I will discover my oneness with another. My self-definition will expand to encompass the other person because I have dropped that which was creating a duality.

All of this is pertinent to becoming one with others through love and service, as well as one with ourself. Amazingly, many of us do not have a sense of oneness with ourselves. A frequent problem is not loving the *body*. We may take care of the body *only* because we expect something back from it. We may eat right and exercise *only* so that we will have the energy and stamina we want. However, a real sense of oneness of body, mind and spirit is attained with a different attitude—a desire to give to the body the best we can simply because it is loved and appreciated.

As we expand the boundary of our self-definition to include our own body, mind and spirit, then we can more effectively reach out through selfless service and become one with others. To insure that our reaching out is not merely to gain approval from a third party or even to get something back from the other person, we should try whenever possible to do our acts of love *anonymously*. We should not limit ourselves only to anonymous love, but nevertheless be on the lookout for using this method whenever we can.

Experiment: Give of yourself and your resources to others without expectation of something back. Find ways to be of loving service to others without their knowing who has been the source of the aid.

Chapter Nine
KNOWLEDGE

"We have knowledge when we seek to express less and less of self and more and more of God in our dealings with our fellow man..." p. 81

One of the great paradoxes of living in the earth concerns self-development. It is equally true that we are here for our souls to grow and that we are here to serve others. We can never throw away either aspect of the polarity. If we try to serve without a sense of nurturing our inner selves, then our feeble efforts at service never evolve into the profound kind of loving that is possible. If we hide our heads in the sand and just work on our own spiritual attunement, we do two things: First, we shut down the channel through which that spiritual energy wishes to flow; and second, we deny ourselves the very opportunities which can provide us with the most significant spiritual growth.

One Edgar Cayce reading mentions the confusion and dilemma we sometimes seem to face between self-development and service.

That which is so hard to be understood in the minds or experiences of many is that the activities of a soul are for self-development, yet must be selfless in its activity for it, the soul, to develop.   275-39

How is it, then, that we can focus less on ourselves, more on others and at the same time be developing spiritually? To find an answer, it is best to start at the mental level, the dimension where we create our experiences. We can begin by each asking ourselves this question: "How much of the time do I think about myself and how much about others?" This question asks each of us to consider those periods throughout the day when our minds wander off into our own thought worlds or to our kind of inner, mental dialogue. It happens often throughout the day (e.g., while taking a shower in the morning, riding to work, cooking a meal, etc.). In fact, we are off in our own mental world almost every time we are alone, even though we may be doing something in the physical world simultaneously.

Try to remember what it is you have been thinking about lately. What does your mind go to automatically when left to itself? Probably you will find that most, if not all, of its topics of concern have to do with yourself. Yes, these topics may involve others, but aren't they on your mind because of how they affect you? However, perhaps you will also remember a few instances in which you were thinking about others, just out of your love and caring for them. The mind can do this equally well, if we will just *develop the habit* of doing it.

Perhaps this whole process is most graphically illustrated in our mental distractions during meditation. Here we see most clearly the mind's predisposition to wander off into its own thought world. However, thoughts related just to self are usually counterproductive to what we are trying to do in meditation. During these 15 or 20 minutes we attempt to awaken a sense of desiring to serve and to love.

Here is an exercise to try which may help to reorient the mind. Take the first five minutes of your meditation period to pray for others. This should not be confused with the reason for praying for others in the last five minutes of the meditation. In the latter case, it is to share the energy which has been awakened from within us. The purpose of the exercise being suggested now is a mind reorientation. It does two things. It gets us set up for a better and more effective silence period with our affirmation, one in which any thoughts which arise are *more likely* to be about others and in the very spirit of love which the affirmation represents. And, in an equally important way, this exercise can help us carry over into daily, conscious life a tendency to spend a little less time thinking about ourselves and a little more time thinking about others.

Experiment: Try spending the *first* five minutes of your daily meditation period in prayer for others. Use it to orient your mind so that your following period of silence will be more in keeping with an ideal of love and service.

"...we are willing to take a portion of their burden when they are bowed down with the cares of the world." p. 81

There is a simple way in which we can help others with their burdens and their worldly cares. It is simply a willingness to listen to them. Listening is loving. Haven't we all discovered what a powerful expression of love it is to have someone be willing to listen to our own problems?

To be a good listener to others we must first of all genuinely care about people. Listening is not merely the physical act of sitting there and not saying anything while another speaks to you. Other people can tell when you are truly interested and concerned versus those times when you are impatient or preoccupied and appear to be listening but only out of politeness. There are subtle clues that tip off the other person: eye movements, body language, or maybe even the kind of psychic, intuitive communication which happens nonverbally between people.

If we really care about people, then listening comes easily. This is why the first experiment of this chapter is so crucial: practicing the discipline of spending more time thinking lovingly of others. Of course, even if we develop positive habit patterns of really caring about other people, we cannot fully take on the problems of others. That is, we cannot assume responsibility for whatever difficulty people face. Their own souls are faced with a challenge that no one else can properly step in and take over for them. But help is possible and having someone genuinely listen can be a great help.

Haven't we all had the experience? Something is really troubling us and we find a friend who will listen and suddenly we feel much better. The problem is not solved. The friend did not say, "Oh, I'll take care of that for you." In fact, the friend may not have had any idea what you should do next. All that person really did was to care about you and listen. So how did it work? Why was the listening so potent?

First, it may have been the affirmation by another, "I care about you." For many of our problems we feel threatened that people will not care about us or think as highly of us because of this situation we now face. Having someone say (even indirectly), "I love you even though you have this difficulty," may ease a large part of the anxiety and pain associated with that difficulty.

Second, having to explain and talk out a problem may help us to organize our thoughts about the whole matter. Having to communicate feelings and events may help us to objectify and understand them better.

And finally, there is a third, and perhaps most important,

reason why someone listening to our difficulty makes us feel better. It reminds us that the solution will *not* come from a *closed system.* That is, we need help from beyond our conscious, rational selves. If we close ourselves off, then we are stuck in just the box which created the problem in the first place! Ultimately the real solution may come by opening ourselves to inner direction from the higher self or from God. But an *open system* is regained. We may be rehearsing this as we honestly share our concern with another person and observe how he cares about us. For a few minutes at least we have practiced the *process* which can exist between us and God: trust, vulnerability and openness to receive.

Seeing more clearly now how *we* have been helped by others listening to us, let us turn matters around. We can go out into our world and ease the burdens of others by taking the time to really listen to their concerns.

Experiment: Make it a discipline to take some time each day to really listen to what is concerning one or two people. You do not have the answer to their questionings. Just express your love through your attention as they open up and share.

"Knowledge is the ability that enables us to live in harmony with the laws of the universe." p. 81

There are many physical laws which have parallel laws of consciousness. The phrase "living in harmony" suggests one such case: the physical law of resonance. This law concerns the effects of vibratory forces and describes how a sympathetic vibratory pattern can be induced in a second structure.

Probably we are all familiar with an example of this law in action. Strike a tuning fork and bring it into physical proximity with a second tuning fork (one that is structurally similar) and what happens? An identical and "sympathetic" vibratory pattern is induced in the second fork. It begins to vibrate, too, without having been struck. This is the law of resonance.

This law can work just as dramatically with consciousness. In order to understand how, first consider that each day there is an optimal set of items which our soul would like to get done. One Edgar Cayce reading suggests that we start the day by asking, "Lord, what would You have me do this day?" Let us think of that potential to get certain things done today as a sort of vibration, as a type of energy pattern within the soul. Remember that "things to be done" are not just at a material level (e.g., wood to chop, bread to bake, shopping to do), but also "things to be done" with our thoughts and our feelings.

To experience how the law of resonance works, observe how you live your conscious life with a particular *tempo*. It is characterized by how fast your physical movements are and how quickly your mind shifts from one topic to another. Our tempo of living changes from day to day. It is like breathing. If we put our awareness upon it, then we can control it and determine its rate. However, if it is left on its own, its rate will be controlled by circumstances.

The law of resonance, when applied to consciousness, would say this: Each day we can consciously find and maintain a tempo of living which corresponds to what our soul wants to get done today. When the two are matched, then it creates a oneness of structure which allows an energy to be transmitted to our physical lives. It is just as the one tuning fork transmits an energy to the second fork.

You may say, "This sounds fine, but how do I discover what tempo to choose in order to get this unified flow of creative energy? If I do not know what God wants me to do today, how can I select an optimal tempo of moving, thinking and feeling?" The answer often lies in trial and error. You are most likely to confront such trials on days when you don't feel "with it." Perhaps things just keep going wrong or you feel depleted. You need a sense of getting back in harmony or you need a new supply of energy.

This is the time to start experimenting with the tempo of your living that day. It may involve slowing down or speeding up. For example, sometimes when we feel low energy and we are sitting around doing nothing, we need to pick up the tempo. If we consciously start acting and thinking more quickly, we may discover that seemingly out of nowhere we get a burst of enthusiasm and energy. This may be the law of resonance at work. We may have just gotten our tempo "in phase" with what our soul had set as an optimal rhythm for the day.

Some people who are joggers or runners have observed this principle of resonant energy. On a given day they must find a tempo of movement which allows them to run their farthest distance. Sometimes only very small changes in tempo suddenly seem to put them in a groove where it feels as if they could run forever. They must experiment each day to find what that tempo is for that day. We can discover this same law of energy available to us through resonance. It can be applied to all of our aspects of our daily living.

Experiment: Each day try to find a tempo of acting, thinking and feeling which puts you in touch with the tempo your soul wants to get done what it needs. Use that resultant extra energy which becomes available in a creative way.

"We. . .are workmen who are not ashamed of the things that will prove our sincerity and our earnestness." p. 82

The phrase "workmen not ashamed" is quoted many times in the Cayce readings. Undoubtedly it refers to much more than just being proud of ourselves as teachers, homemakers, lawyers or whatever. Looking at the phrase more broadly, what does it mean to be unashamed of the *spiritual work* in which we are involved?

Perhaps it first means that we are not to hide the beliefs and principles by which we live. The automatic human reaction in shame is to want to *hide* that of which one is ashamed. Do we ever hide the beliefs which we hold? It is easier to say to oneself, "I don't want to rock the boat, so I'll just keep quiet about what I believe." However, if we are truly proud of what we believe to be God's laws and His work in the earth, aren't we challenged to speak up and share who we are and in what we have faith?

Yes, there is another principle which speaks of not "casting pearls before swine" (a Biblical figure of speech which seems a bit distasteful to some of us who don't want to be put in the position of judging someone else to be "swine"). However, the key word in that phrase may be "pearls." We don't *start* by sharing our most personal, precious spiritual experience with someone who may not be ready to understand what it has meant to us. But we may be most wise and loving to cast "food to swine" or to any living being whom we seek to love.

So why is it that many of us draw back from claiming or admitting to our belief system? Many of its tenets are still unorthodox in our society. The majority of people do not meditate, do not study dreams and certainly do not accept reincarnation as a working hypothesis. We stand to be ridiculed or thought to be unusual by taking the initiative to share our perspective of the world.

And yet, over and over, Edgar Cayce's readings said, "Do not be ashamed." In other words, do not hide who you really are and in what you really believe. We can risk the fact that there will be a few people who will think less of us. If we do our sharing with proper timing and sensitivity, there will be more people who are glad we opened up and told them of our philosophies and disciplines.

Experiment: Try to let go of any embarrassment or uncomfortableness you may experience with the spiritual things you believe even though people who are "worldly wise" may think you foolish, impractical or naive. Be willing earnestly and sincerely to share aspects of the spiritual path you are on. With sensitivity and an eye toward proper timing take the initiative in such sharing.

"The knowledge of God does not bind us to dogmas, or man-made beliefs; rather it sets us free." p. 82

This passage defines a contrast between freedom and dogma. It suggests that if we wish to experience freedom—at any level, physical, mental or spiritual—one place to begin is an observation of where dogma controls our lives. This certainly extends well beyond questions of whether or not we accept orthodox religious teachings. The most crucial area is *self-imposed* dogma which prevents our own freedom.

It is the *rigidity* of dogma which is so paralyzing. Humankind may indeed need boundaries and forms in which to grow. But when those boundaries and forms grab control of our lives rather than serve us, then we find that a sense of freedom is lost.

Perhaps our own most limiting dogmas are our routines. We fall into thinking that we have to live our lives a certain way. A patterned way of getting something done may have started out as an aid to help us use our time more economically. But we can fall prey to that pattern; rigidity sets in and it becomes a fixed routine. Our sense of creativity and of alternatives is lost, and with it our sense of freedom is gone.

The answer is to identify our routines and *periodically* prove to ourselves that we are not under their power. Break a patterned way that you perform daily actions. Do some things which are out of the ordinary for you. By doing this you open up to parts of yourself and ways of being with which you have been out of touch.

There is the potential of a tremendous impact upon your awareness and self-knowledge in making these simple changes. For example, if it is your routine to eat a particular breakfast, periodically try a totally different morning diet. If you always wear your billfold in your left pocket, put it in your right pocket for a week. If you always shower in the morning, shower before bedtime for a few days.

These are not just games, despite their appearance. The simple examples just cited (or ones like them which you decide for yourself) are intended to be catalysts. They are meant to start a process of awareness into action which will, in turn, uncover deeper levels of dogma. We rigidly hold to a wide variety of feelings and thoughts, too. Our spiritual freedom can be impaired by any ingrained routine which controls us.

Experiment: Pick several routine actions in your life. For a period of several days experience your freedom from that patterned way of living your life by finding alternatives to those actions.

"If we would know God, we must experience God; and as we experience Him, we become a god to someone else." p. 84

Perhaps it sounds a little intimidating or audacious to consider being a god to someone else. You may, however, begin by trying to be the best person you can be toward another individual. It means showing to him or her all the different qualities and talents which make you a whole person.

We all have within ourselves a concept of who we would like to be and how we would like to be known to others. And usually this concept varies somewhat from the sort of person which most people think of us as being. We long for a fresh start in some relationships because once we are known to be a certain way, it is difficult to show another side of ourselves without being thought unusual or being teased.

For example, consider a businesswoman who is very bright and well organized. After months or even years of interacting with people at her job, she realizes that they have a very definite image of her. They see her as intelligent, ambitious and very disciplined. However, she knows that there are other important sides of her that she has never shown them. She knows that there is as well an intuitive, free-flowing part of her soul. Perhaps in the past she has never felt quite as comfortable with this other side and, therefore, had never learned very effective ways of letting it out for others to experience.

But let us say that now she wishes to communicate herself to others as a whole person. It may be very difficult at first to reveal her hidden side to those who have known her for a long time. She expects that they would tease her when she first begins to act in ways that are unusual to them. However, imagine that a new employee comes to work at the company. This person knows nothing of her character. This relationship can be like a beginning—for the first time she can comfortably let this new employee get to know her as a whole person. She does not have to fight her own past expectations or his.

This story suggests a discipline for each of us to try. Every time we start a new relationship with another person it is a beautiful opportunity. That person does not have preconceived expectations about what qualities you have and what qualities you lack. Even if a mutual friend has previously talked about you to that person, he or she still has no experiences with you yet. Here is an opportunity to be most fully the kind of person you have wanted others to know you as being. Here is the chance to be a whole person to someone else.

Experiment: Make a list of two or three qualities which *you* know are in you but others may not know about because you rarely, if ever, expose them. Select ones which you would like to reveal more often (e.g., a sense of humor, a serious side, warmth, a good organizer, a good listener). When you start up a new relationship, try to show two or three of these qualities *early* in your experiences together.

"What is applicable to an individual is applicable to groups. It is like leaven; it leavens the whole." p. 85

The work of transforming consciousness on this planet seems overwhelming. When you read or listen to the news, it is staggering to realize what a small percentage of humanity operates from a spiritual awareness or has any kind of spiritual ideal. How can the effort of just a handful, relatively speaking, bring about the changes which are needed? There are examples in history (e.g., the few early Christians), but what is the law which allows this to take place?

Edgar Cayce's phrase in referring to this process was "the little leaven which leavens the whole lump." In other words, an individual can lift the consciousness of even a large group; and groups can lift the consciousness of the masses. It is almost like the physical principle of leverage. We can exert a greatly magnified effect on an object by properly using a lever.

Perhaps another meaning of the phrase would be "God gives the increase." For each unit of time or energy expended in doing God's work, it may be that a ten- or even hundredfold effect is transmitted into the material plane, either directly through us or even indirectly at various points around the globe.

We might think of the process in terms of a fund-raising analogy. Some large donor or perhaps the state government has promised to give five or even ten dollars for every dollar contributed by an alumnus. When we hear about such a program at our own school, it sounds very encouraging. It says that for a little effort on our part we can induce a far greater impact than normally expected. Our $10 check may really mean a $100 income for the school.

Where in daily life can we look to have such a leavening effect? No place is better than the *groups* to which we belong. Many people have predicted that the New Age will be a period of the group. Leadership may come out of groups rather than single individuals. Spiritual growth may be viewed as a function of group work rather than the isolated hermit meditating on the mountaintop.

What are the groups to which you belong, either formal groups (church, family, study group, speakers club, etc.) or loosely defined groups (work groups, circles of friends, etc.)? Begin to observe how the practicing of your ideals can have *a leavening effect on other members of the group.* Simply share by example the spiritual awareness you are developing. It is through such a commitment to the groups of which we are members that we may be able to do our greatest work in lifting consciousness on this planet.

Experiment: Identify three or four specific groups of which you are a member (e.g., your family, your work group, your study group, your circle of friends). Try to be a leaven to the consciousness and awareness of the group. Through what you say and do help to direct the flow of energies of each group in the most constructive, hopeful way possible.

"Kindness is a simple act, but it is great enough to express divine knowledge." p. 84

"A kind word under trying circumstances not only creates for us an attunement with the 'I Am' but makes others aware of the presence of the Lord." p. 86

What is the relationship between knowledge and kindness? One aspect of the interaction of these two qualities can be found in our own intimate personal relationships.

Think for a moment about the areas where you most desire kindness from others. Aren't many of them the very relationships with people who know you best? Isn't there a measure of vulnerability which comes from being known—and known in many of your secret corners—by another person? It is the person who knows your darkest side (your fears, your guilts, your worries) who can potentially hurt you the most with a thoughtless remark or unnecessary criticism.

Realizing this, we can then turn the tables and see where it is most important to be kind ourselves. Certainly we want to continue to try to be kind to strangers, but the place our kindness is needed most is among those whom we know best. That is where a lack of kindness can do the most harm. And unfortunately, many of us slip into taking for granted the people whom we know the best. Family members and beloved friends are often the people whom we see most often. There may be the tendencies to forget the psychological and spiritual vulnerabilities which are felt by these people who have allowed us to know them so well.

This is not to say that we must always give such people exactly what they want for fear of hurting their feelings. In fact one Edgar Cayce reading speaks to this issue saying: "And remember, a kindness sometimes consists in denying as well as granting those activities in associations with thy fellow man." (5322-1)

What is needed in order to be kind—no matter what form of expression it takes—is to be sensitive and aware. Our greatest responsibilities in this area are to those who have allowed us to know them best.

Experiment: Consider the relationships in your life about which you have the most knowledge. These are probably ones of trust in which the individuals have been able to share with you deep and important things about themselves. It is likely that they are also the relationships in which you can most easily hurt the other person. For a week make a special effort to be kind—in word and action—to one of these people.

Chapter Ten

WISDOM

"Wisdom is the ability to use knowledge aright. It is made practical by the application of the Christ life in our daily experiences." p. 91

Simply stated, knowledge can be understood as the *awareness* of aspects of reality; whereas wisdom is the *application* of that awareness in material life. We may, for example, know a principle of human psychology and yet not be wise enough to use it properly in our interactions with others.

There are, of course, many aspects to the development of wisdom. In this experiment let us focus on just one: the relationship between wisdom and *proper timing*. We all have had experiences that did not turn out as we had hoped and yet we are sure that what we did or said was true.

For example, imagine a man who has fallen in love with a woman who is going through a divorce. Once he becomes aware of his feelings and aware of the good friendship they seem to have, he may be tempted to tell her right away of his love for her. And yet, the best application of that knowledge may not be to say such a thing right away. If he is wise he will find the proper timing. If he tries to act on his knowledge too soon, she may not be ready to consider another close relationship at that moment. His knowledge might be "right"—i.e., their compatibility has the potential to grow into something more—but if it is expressed with improper timing it might undermine any future chance for their relationship to grow.

What this means is that wisdom requires *sensitivity*. Whereas knowledge may be absolute (i.e., one either knows something or he does not know it), wisdom is more relative—it exists within the context of events. To be wise we must not only ask ourselves, "Is what I am about to do or say true?" but also ask, "Is this the best moment to do or say this?"

We might think of all this by way of a music analogy. We may have knowledge of how to sing the note middle C. However, when do we choose to sing that note? If events or people around us at a given moment are "singing" F sharp and A flat, we shall contribute to a discordant sound. However, if the events or people are "singing" the notes E and G, we shall have contributed to a beautiful chord. That is a significant aspect of wisdom.

Experiment: Pay attention to the *timing* of when you say things you know are true or do things which you know are right.

"The fear of the Lord is the beginning of wisdom." p. 91

If God is love, how can we speak of the fear of the Lord? Perhaps what is meant by "fear" is not the emotional reaction of self-protection in a threatening situation. Instead, we are being encouraged to *respect* God.

And just what does respect for God entail? Once again our tendency might be to think of respect in the same context as the respect we have for fire or a big dog. We are cautious, knowing that there is always the possibility of being hurt. This is what we often call a "healthy respect." In other words, for our own health or well-being, either we steer clear of that person or object or we deal with it very gingerly.

However, this notion of "healthy respect" does not seem to fit the sort of relationship we are invited to have with God. Instead, there is another view of respect and it concerns the scope or the range of God's involvement in our lives. Many times we fail to respect God fully because we only bring Him into our lives for the big problems. Certainly we are quick to turn to prayer when we face a major crisis. But do we also remember to invite the Spirit to guide and strengthen us in the *little* events of daily life? If we respect God, then we see His scope or His range of involvement in every aspect of human life. The "fear of the Lord" may mean the awareness of God's constant presence and involvement in everything that we do.

In order to grow in this awareness—to grow in this aspect of wisdom—we can make it a discipline to remember God, not just in our regular prayer and meditation periods, but in every element of human life. How can you invite God's presence into your awareness during housecleaning, garden work, office work, love-making, eating and all the other big and little parts of your life? The beginning of wisdom is the fear of the Lord: respect for the range and scope of God's involvement with us.

Experiment: With your thoughts bring God and your spiritual ideal into one area which you may have thought was too trivial *or* too human for His concern. One way to do this is simply to have short periods of prayer while you are involved in that activity.

"Our Lord taught that: If thy brother smite thee, turn the other cheek; if he takes away thy coat, let him have thy cloak also; if he forces thee to go one mile, go with him two. In such teaching there is wisdom, for we are not hindered by the act, while our brother is blessed by being in the presence of the Divine." p. 91

A second important aspect of wisdom is not to be hindered by the acts or appearances of what others do. The particular teaching of Jesus referred to in the passage just quoted is one of the most difficult to apply. It seems to invite other people to take advantage of us. However, if we want to look at it from the perspective of an invitation, it actually invites us to see beyond the material appearances of things and sense the mental and spiritual realities of life.

This notion of "do not judge by appearances" is central not only to wisdom but to the entire spiritual path. We must be in a material world, yes—we must *deal* with appearances, but not confine our evaluations and judgments to them only. It is unrealistic to simply say "do not judge," because in fact we must make evaluations and judgments in order to function. If we are to follow Jesus' teachings, though, here is how we must do it: "Do not judge by appearances, but judge with right judgment." (John 7:24) And "right judgment" seems to suggest a kind of sensitivity to what is going on at mental and spiritual levels.

Wisdom looks for feedback on what it has done; it looks for the fruits of its actions. However, that "looking" is not just at physical appearances. Instead there can be fruits at other levels and they may be missed if we are looking only for material results.

When we perform the right action, it does not always make

119

things appear physically better at first—and may, in fact, make them appear physically worse for awhile. The wise person knows about and uses this principle. In applying what he knows to be true, the wise person is sensitive to the fruits of what has been done, but does not look merely at the material appearances.

We have all seen or heard of examples of this process. The alcoholic who decides to stop drinking may go through horrendous-looking physical symptoms as his body readjusts. If we judged only by appearances, we might think that he was not wise in giving up his drinking. However, the fruits are immediately apparent at mental and spiritual levels in the resolve and determination to apply his ideal.

Another example is the person with financial problems who decides to try economic healing principles. She might give to someone in greater need out of the little money she has left. Temporarily that seems to make things worse if we judge only her action and the appearances. However, in her wisdom she realizes that something else is happening to her attitudes and her spiritual ideal.

Experiment: Do the right thing when the timing is right, even if by appearances things may seem to be a bit worse at first. Use wisdom to evaluate and judge fruits at all levels.

Examples: Give up a habit you have been wanting to eliminate even though at first it may make you very uncomfortable; or, communicate an emotion you have been keeping bottled up inside you, even though at first it may seem to weaken your relationship to the person you tell.

"There is no shortcut to wisdom; it must be lived." p. 92

One human characteristic which is often confused with wisdom is the intellect. There are times in which we may be so impressed with how smart a person is that we slip into assuming that that individual is wise as well. For example, imagine a woman who has read all the books to be found on organic gardening. Intellectually she may have absorbed all the facts. She may possess tremendous book knowledge and answer our every question about types of seeds, planting times, soil nutrients, etc. However, she may never have planted a garden. She may lack the wisdom that comes from having *lived* those facts.

The intellect can become the vehicle for taking shortcuts. As important as it can be for accumulating knowledge, it can stand as an obstacle to growth into wisdom. The reason for this lies in the capability of logic, a prime tool of the intellect. Logic often allows the user to predetermine what the results will be without having to carry out physically all the intervening steps. Properly used, it makes life much more efficient. It permits us to avoid costly and unnecessary mistakes and squandering of personal resources. However, taken to an extreme, it goes so far as to be an avoidance of actually dealing with the materiality of life.

In our example, the woman may be an "armchair gardener." Using her imagination and logic, she may plant many gardens and see what the logical results will be of a wide variety of gardening techniques. However, the work of the soul is to *spiritualize matter* and she cannot do this unless she gets *involved* in *living* all of her book knowledge.

Are there ways in which you use the intellect and its tool of logic to take shortcuts? Do you ever find yourself saying, "I know it would be good for me to do that"? *Our* shortcuts may be more *subtle* than the blatant use of intellect and logic by the armchair gardener; but the principle remains the same. Of course, we do not need to act out and live the knowledge we have of what produces bad results. Logic can help us avoid those efforts. The gardener doesn't have to live out those items which she knows will ruin a garden. However, since wisdom comes in spiritualizing the physical dimension, that which we intellectually know to produce good results needs to be acted upon and lived.

Experiment: Eliminate shortcuts to wisdom which employ a misuse of intellect and logic. Select something which your intellect tells you will likely lead to good results in the physical plane (e.g., diet or a certain way of behaving with others). Probably it's something you have been *thinking about doing* for some time, but you already know how it will turn out. Now try living it.

"For as ye apply day by day that ye know, then is the next step, the next act, the next experience, shown thee." p. 94

One of the unique features of the *A Search for God* material is its growth-sequence quality. That is, the insights gained from one lesson topic often provide a key to a better understanding of the next one. This chapter on wisdom is a good example, as it follows the one on knowledge.

The way in which *A Search for God* reflects a growth sequence is only a shadow of the way in which life itself is an orderly pattern of learning, building sequentially step by step. Of course, a common error which we make is to try to complete a step before it is required of us.

Much of our *worrying* is related to a misunderstanding of the way in which life teaches us. It can be illustrated by the following diagram.

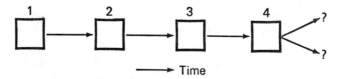

When we are at position number one we may suspect that in the future we will be at position number four and have to make some kind of a choice. However, the choice does not really exist now (i.e., at position number one). Unfortunately, we may worry about that future decision now, and be concerned that we may make a wrong choice then. We may forget that there will be intervening experiences (i.e., numbers two and three) between now and the time when the choice finally has to be made. Those intervening experiences will each provide some type of growth and learning. We will *not be the same person* at point number four as we are at point number one. In other words, we should make only choices which need to be made today. If a decision which will have to be faced somewhere down the road does not have a clear answer to you today, that is all right. There will be learning and change on your part. Quite likely by the time the choice really does have to be made, you will have learned something that will make the decision far easier.

Experiment: Make only those *decisions* which need to be made today. If you find yourself worrying about a future decision, try to reorient your attitude. Trust that when the time comes when you really will have to choose, then you will know what to do. Pray that experience and necessary guidance will be shown to you between now and the time you have to decide.

"Try in thine own experience, that ye speak not for one whole day unkindly of any, that ye say not a harsh word to any, about any, and see what the day would bring to you." p. 94

As we develop wisdom, we realize that speaking unkindly of any person or situation does little to help it. In fact it is the wise person who can see and can follow a course of action which is effective, which contributes to positive change and greater wholeness. We can anticipate that harsh words will not do that.

How then are we to behave as we develop our capacity to look at people and situations with greater insight? As we learn more and more about universal law and the spiritual destiny of every soul, then we are more likely to notice where others (and ourselves) are falling short. How does a person with developing wisdom react in a situation where once he or she might have harshly criticized another or spoken unkindly of someone?

The first question we must answer is this: Do we *genuinely* want that person or situation to be healed and whole? Just because we may have criticized a situation or spoken harshly of someone does not necessarily mean that we care very much about healing taking place. Do we derive a sort of pleasure or emotional entertainment from this other person's shortcoming or that disruptive situation? We will not be able to act out of wisdom unless we first get clear about a sincere desire to have conditions be better.

However, when and if we discover this sincere desire to help, then we can try to apply one of the great marks of wisdom: Allow the situation to reveal itself. In other words, the wise person is able to act in a way that coaxes the truth to the surface. Wisdom does not always know the answer but knows what to do so that life will yield its secrets.

A great Biblical model of wisdom is Solomon, and the classic example of his wisdom concerned the two women who both claimed to be the mother of a single baby. Solomon did not know the answer to this dilemma nor did he try to force his opinion or arbitrary decision upon the situation. He did not deal with the women by harsh words, hoping that the one who was a liar would change her behavior because of his unkind treatment. Instead he acted in a way which allowed the truth to reveal itself. In wisdom he threatened to cut the baby in half, knowing that that threat would bring to the surface the truth.

How could we apply this same process? What is the truth of the matter that needs to come to the surface? Consider the person of whom you are inclined to speak harshly. If you are right and that person is doing somthing wrong, then you can still trust that life will bring that person face to face with his shortcomings. Your unkind words are not required to insure that he won't get away with anything. On the other hand, there is also a deeper level of truth within that person, a potential self which is whole and healed. As you act with wisdom, you do things which help bring that to the surface.

Consider this hypothetical situation. Suppose you learned that a friend was cheating on his income taxes. Do you spread the word to other friends? Do you speak of his behavior in harsh, unkind terms? In wisdom and a desire to see his life whole, you might do otherwise. Perhaps he is acting out of anger or out of a sense of financial insecurity for the future. He does not need you to preach to him, but there may be wise statements you can make or actions to take which will help draw his real self to the surface of his awareness. You may be able to help him get in touch with the level of himself which knows that it is at peace or knows that there is no need to fear.

Experiment: At *least* for one day go through the whole day without speaking unkindly of anyone. When you feel tempted to speak unkindly about a shortcoming of someone, remember that it is not up to you to make that person face up to himself. You may be right—that fault may be there. Instead, remember your sincere desire to see that person be whole and healed. Act or speak out of wisdom in such a way that it helps bring to the surface that person's wholeness.

"It is the application of that thou knowest to do *in light of the Pattern set in the Christ. That is* applied *Wisdom!" p. 95*

There are many qualities of the Christ pattern that reflect wisdom. Yet perhaps none is more important than the way in which Jesus fulfilled the role that He was meant to play. No doubt He was often tempted to play other roles, to fulfill other potentialities which were within His grasp. He could have been a splendid political leader, full of wisdom, oratory strengths and sensitivity to people. He could have been a fine father, loving children as He did. And yet He chose to be obedient to the boundaries of His life's purposefulness. He chose to maximize how creative He could be within the meaningful limitations of His life's pattern.

Each of us needs that same kind of wisdom. Yes, we need to explore our potentials. We need to discover just what the boundaries are for the purposefulness we have chosen in this particular incarnation. But then we must also accept our limitations and not compare ourselves to others. We each have a unique role to fulfill well. The degree to which we are doing this cannot be measured by what someone else has accomplished.

Try to be at peace with yourself and do not condemn yourself for whatever limitations you have. Within the boundaries of those limitations (if they are honest ones and not born of laziness) all of your spiritual work can be perfectly completed. For example, if you are an office worker and your skills are suited to that, it may well be that your optimum service can best be performed right at that level. You need not feel inadequate if you have not been promoted to supervisor or manager. If you are a jogger and feel better after your one-mile run, do not compare yourself to a neighbor who runs five miles a day. Work instead within the parameters of your own unique character and body. There is great wisdom in being able to do this.

One amazing fact about the Cayce life readings bears out this same principle. We find it by looking at the readings in which individuals were told that this could well be their last incarnation on earth. These people were not famous spiritual teachers. They were often humble, loving individuals with many limitations. What made them special was that in wisdom they learned to fulfill their work within meaningful boundaries. Perhaps no two of us have the same boundaries in which we operate. But we can all try to emulate the wisdom of Jesus—to follow the *process* which His example demonstrates.

Experiment: Where in your life have you honestly explored your capabilities and discovered the boundaries or limits which are unique to you (e.g., in physical exercise, areas of intellectual study, capabilities in your work, talent and skill in the home, etc.)? For those areas where you know of the boundaries which are *now* best for you, try living within them as best you can without any sense of inadequacy, self-criticism or comparison with others.

Chapter Eleven
HAPPINESS

"We manifest. . .[happiness] in thankfulness. . ." p. 99

How often have we said to ourselves over the years, "If only I were happier in my life, then I would be so thankful." And yet too easily a sincere feeling of thankfulness to God is missing when those periods come in which we are happy. Instead, we are more likely to turn to God only when we are in trouble and in need of help.

It is a curious phenomenon of human nature, this tendency to associate God so readily with times of difficulty, stress and need. Perhaps it is akin to our predisposition to take a spiritual law and state it in the negative. For example, we are more likely to think of the law of karma in terms of how it can create our troubles, instead of remembering that through the law of karma the attributes we develop now will carry over. Similarly, we are more likely to say, "The faults of others which bother you most are your *own* worst faults or you wouldn't recognize them," instead of, "The qualities you *admire* in others are within you as well or else you wouldn't recognize them."

It is this curious human habit which may keep us from being thankful to God when we are happy. We are like teenagers who want to think of themselves as free and independent when everything is going well and they are happy. But as soon as there is a big problem in their lives they run to their parents for help. When things are going well for us, it is so easy to just flow with and enjoy life. We may feel that, in fact, we rightly deserve the good things coming our way. The principle, "we can do nothing of ourselves," may be far from our minds.

A good discipline for us is to remember *frequently* to thank God for our blessings when we are happy. We *can* remember the Source of all good when things are going well, not merely when we feel cut off from good and want to get back in touch with that source.

It is just as important to thank God when we are happy as it is to know we can turn to Him for help when we are unhappy and in need of help. Thankfulness keeps us honest; it avoids the one *potential pitfall* of happiness: the belief that *independently* we have created good in our lives.

Experiment: Bring God into the happy moments of your life. During the day, when you have periods of feeling happy, remember the role that God is always playing in your life. With this recognition and remembrance, or with the words of a short prayer, be thankful.

"Happy are the meek. . .Those who are quiet, cool and unpretentious are the makers and the keepers of the coming age who will bring light and understanding to many." p. 99

In our modern world it sometimes seems that to get anything done—or even to be heard at all—we must be loud and aggressive. In the midst of hard-sell marketing and people busier than they have ever been before, how can you get through unless you are assertive? Meekness, like obedience, hardly seems to have a place in our world. And if you want to get something done, it almost seems foolish to be meek, unpretentious or quiet.

So what is the promise that the meek shall inherit the earth or that the unpretentious are the makers and keepers of the coming age? It seems just as paradoxical a teaching now as it did in the Roman era when Jesus proposed it. However, perhaps this teaching asks us to redefine what it means to *control* the earth and what does it mean to get things *done*.

Who is the heir to this planet? Who controls things here in the dimension of living? *A person who does not have self-control certainly has no real control over events in his own life or the lives of anyone else.* Did Pilate really have control over Jesus who was acting in a meek and unpretentious way? Of course not.

Despite appearances, some of the quiet and unpretentious people who may have gained a measure of self-mastery are, in fact, in an actual position to lead the world and create new alternatives for our planet. Many who now appear to be in control of events are actually being controlled themselves. We should never let behavior which seems aggressive or pushy communicate to us that such a person is in control. Often such behavior in people is the result of quite the opposite—they are anxious about *being controlled*.

So if we are to be the real leaders and builders of the future world, we must progress in a way which by appearance may seem to relinquish importance and authority. We can be unpretentious out of strength, not out of fear or self-doubt. We can be quiet and meek because we have developed self-control, not because we think others are better than we. There is nothing impotent or weak about meekness when it comes from a centered place within ourselves. There is nothing lost in turning the limelight away from ourselves when we already know and love ourselves. It is this kind of meekness and unpretentiousness which is uniquely able to inherit leadership and control of this dimension of God's creation.

Experiment: Make an effort to be more unpretentious and quiet in your daily affairs. Ask others about themselves and turn the limelight *away from you*.

"What we give away, we have, is as true as what we hold, we lose, or what we have lost was never ours." p. 100

Surrender is a principle which is required of us in so many aspects of spiritual growth. In meditation we must be able to surrender not only distractions which come up but also surrender preconceptions about what we might receive in that particular meditation period. In the development of psychic and intuitive abilities, many people have reported that they had to let go of trying in order to be successful. And in human relations we also need to nurture a capacity to release and surrender those we love.

In fact one of the great qualities of love is its ability to grant freedom to another person. Probably we have all discovered in our own ways that clinging to someone stifles real love in the relationship. Temporarily it may keep the other person around, but the quality of the relationship deteriorates.

If we love someone we must continually have a sense of being willing to let that person go. This does *not* mean a willingness to toss away commitments, vows or promises in the relationship. "Willing to let him *go*" will mean only occasionally the actual departure of that person. More often the phrase means willing to let him *grow* in the way he chooses rather than in the way we want him to.

Of course, this is not always easy. It demands that we be concerned first with the quality of relationship a loved one has *with himself or herself.* In real love we continually surrender our own preoccupation with how that other person is relating to us and grant that loved one the freedom to get straight with self first.

The perspective of loving was put forth by Steward Emery in an article entitled, "Making Your Relationships Work." He wrote: "Love is when I am concerned with your relationship with your own life, rather than with your relationship to mine." The beauty of all this lies in the realization that you and I are not going to have a quality love relationship unless we both have strong love for ourselves first. Surrender and letting go permits the environment of freedom in which this can happen.

Experiment: Work with an attitude of surrender in relation to the various people in your life whom you love. Grant them (by your words and your actions) a sense of freedom to grow in the way they think best. Put their relations with *themselves* before their relationship with you.

" 'Let not your heart be troubled, neither let it be afraid.' In the world of uneasiness and turmoils, this is a happy state of consciousness. . ." p. 100

Our times are times of uncertainty. Perhaps never before in recorded history have events changed so rapidly as they have in the past several decades. In many ways the human being was not built to live in such rapidly changing conditions. And the stress which changing times places upon us now will most likely only increase in the coming years.

The development of our ability to cope with the turmoils and uneasiness we see constantly around us is probably our greatest challenge. Dr. Carl Rogers, a pioneer in humanistic psychology, calls this issue a problem far greater than nuclear weapons or the population explosion. In a paper entitled "Interpersonal Relationships: USA 2000," he writes: "Can [mankind] keep up with the ever-increasing rate of techno-logical change, or is there some point at which the human organism goes to pieces?"

Perhaps the answer to Dr. Rogers' question lies at least partially in this principle: Times of uneasiness and turmoil bring out either the best or the worst in us. In other words, stress and change have a polarizing effect. We will observe this in both our individual lives and in the society at large. On some days, the difficulties of these times will bring out our worst side of impatience, skepticism and worry. And yet on other days, when we are coming from a more centered place, the same outer conditions can stimulate us to faith and never-before-used inner resources. In our society we can expect to see in the coming ten to twenty years a polarizing into two communities: people of faith and hope versus people of fear and worry.

Of course, our job is to try to maintain membership in that first group. One way in which we do this is by responding creatively to daily life situations which present uneasiness and turmoil. Our challenge and opportunity is to not let our hearts be troubled.

One direct way of doing this is to remember continually that it is God who does the work—we are merely His messengers and servants. So often we are harried, tense and overburdened by the stresses and turmoils of these times. We just do not know how we can find the time or energy to get necessary things done. Or we worry about conditions outside our own control (the weather, delayed airplanes, etc.).

The following affirmation can help us in such times: "If God needs me to get this thing done, He will provide the means." Of course the affirmation works only if we have sincerely been trying to do the best we can. However, properly used it is a powerful statement of faith. It can lift us out of stress and a troubled heart. It redefines the priorities of our lives by saying that which is really important to us is what God wants us to get done today and we trust that He has the power to see that we can do it. In that feeling of release, trust and faith, we may find happiness even in the middle of uneasy and stressful times.

Experiment: Observe the moments in which you let the turmoils and uneasiness of these times get to you. It may be the hectic pace or the continual state of things changing. Whenever you begin to feel troubled or tense that certain things may be blocked which you feel you need to get done, then use the affirmation: "If God needs me to get this thing done, He will provide the means." Let the affirmation lift you to a new attitude of faith, trust and happiness about your life.

"When the Lord's will becomes our will, we are happy, for we begin to know the Lord in our daily life." p. 101

The relationship between human free will and happiness is a central issue in the philosophy of the *A Search for God* approach. Since we were children, we have had the notion that somehow being free to do whatever we want to do makes us happy. Unfortunately the very experience of realizing we *do* have free will makes us happier than do the results of most choices we make with that free will. In other words, we may feel exhilarated to know that we can do and be whatever we want; however, our choice of what we are going to do and be often leads us to unhappiness.

In a fine passage on the meaning of will from Eula Allen's Creation Trilogy, this relationship between happiness and our capacity to choose freely is stressed:

"So soon as man contemplates his free will he thinks of it as a means of doing the opposite of God's will, though he finds that only by doing God's will does he find happiness. Yet, the notion of serving God sits ill with him, for he sees it as a sacrifice of his [own] will. Only in disillusion and suffering, in time, space, and patience, does he come to the wisdom that his real will is the will of God, and in its practice is happiness and heaven."

(Allen, *Before the Beginning,* p. 18)

This passage seems to be saying that we have a tendency to view the freedom with which the will provides us as a freedom to go apart from God. Often for us it is hard to see how obedience and freedom can be linked. And yet the feedback which our experience provides us strongly indicates that this is in fact the case—serving God and maintaining a sense of free will are not incompatible. Furthermore, the very essence of happiness is found in knowing that we are doing just what God planned for us to be doing.

Experiment: Focus for several days on especially trying to make choices which you intuitively feel are the ones which reflect God's will for your life. Make use of your own sense of fulfillment, rightness and happiness as a criterion for evaluating the choices you have made.

"Moments of discouragement will arise in our experience. We may expect them; such seem necessary for our training." p. 101

Discouragement is a response we may have to things which are not going the way we had hoped and planned. Sometimes we become discouraged because situations outside our own control do not seem to turn out right. However, there are other times when we become discouraged with our own failures.

Perhaps the most paralyzing kind of discouragement is the result of feeling guilty. We have set an ideal and then have failed to live up to it. Guilt does not have to be our reaction to having failed to meet an ideal. But often it is, and in such cases we frequently experience discouragement.

For example, a woman may have set an ideal of tolerance instead of criticism for the way she thinks about her child. And if she finds herself continuing to be negative and critical towards that child, she may begin to experience guilt. Guilt is the awareness of having failed to live up to a standard. It is also an attitudinal and emotional response which belittles and rejects the aspect of oneself which was involved.

The woman in our example needs to be aware of having failed to live up to a standard. Unless she can evaluate herself, she will never grow. Nevertheless, she does not necessarily need to *condemn* that part of herself which failed. When she does this, she feels guilty; and when she continually feels guilty, she is likely to become very discouraged with herself. She may find herself saying, "I'll just never be able to improve my relationship with my child."

Since guilt is often the source of discouragement, then perhaps the answer to overcoming discouragement is to catch it at this point of origin. A method for doing this involves ideals, but it is an area of ideals which is usually forgotten. However, without the missing area of ideals having been set, we have done only half the job. And we leave ourselves especially open for discouragement.

That missing area is to set ideals for our relationship with the "failing part of self." Just as we can set ideals for relationships with John, Mary and the neighbor next door, we can set mental and physical ideals for that part of ourselves which has failed to live up to some of our other ideals. It is analogous to the spare tire in your car. You buy the best tires you can, but occasionally one of them will fail and get flat. Then you had better have a reliable replacement for that failure. Otherwise you will just sit by the roadside feeling discouraged and going nowhere. Many of us are out traveling on our spiritual journey with no reliable spare tire.

In order to set these often overlooked ideals, we can ask ourselves these two questions:

(1) Mental ideal: What are the best attitudes I can have toward myself when I have failed to live up to my other ideals? (For example, do I react with frustration, anger and self-condemnation or do I react with patience and self-forgiveness? Choose the words which represent your mental ideals.)

(2) Physical ideal: What is the best thing for me to *do* when I discover I have failed in living up to my other ideals? (For example, is it to withdraw and sulk? Or is it to pray about the situation, go out and do something creative or go out and get some physical exercise? Choose the words which represent your physical ideals.)

These ideals—so often ignored—can be the answer to a large part of our discouragement with self. Anyone seriously on the spiritual path is going to have days when he or she falls short and fails. These special ideals you have just set can be a powerful tool to keep you going without long delays of discouragement.

Experiment: Write down physical and mental ideals for your relationship with yourself when it fails. Try using and applying these ideals as a way of minimizing feelings of discouragement with yourself.

"We should find happiness in just sowing the seed." p. 103

Sowing seeds of hope and understanding in the lives of others is a profound expression of love. With a little act or word which reflects truth, we may stimulate that in another person which will grow into something far greater weeks or even years later. No doubt, we all know how important this can be because we have been on the receiving end. We have been the soil in which friends, loved ones and teachers have planted their seeds. Now, many of these seeds have become the source of the best fruits of our lives.

Think about your life and observe areas in which you have been the beneficiary of seeds which were sown. In some cases don't you find that the person who planted the seed in you is no longer in your life? Perhaps that person never got a chance to see the good which came as a result of the little things which were said or done. Those people may be dead or may have moved away. Or perhaps you were acquainted with them for only a brief time. But, no doubt, you are thankful that the seeds were planted.

The realization of how we have been helped ourselves in this manner should encourage us to express love in the same way. It takes a great faith in people just to plant seeds. We usually want people to accept fully and wholeheartedly the wisdom and understanding we have. It takes great faith in the rich soil of the human soul just to plant a thought or idea.

Perhaps the greatest obstacle to any act of love—including seed planting—is that we want something in return. And there are very subtle desires within us for getting something back. Some people insist on seeing for themselves the sprouting, growth and fruition of their seeds. The reward they want back is not attention or money, but it is the good feeling they get from seeing another person change for the better.

Certainly there is nothing wrong with having such good feelings. The problem, however, arises if we refuse to plant seeds when there is clearly little prospect of ever seeing how they turn out. If it is unlikely that we will ever get this particular reward, does that mean the act of love is refused?

Each day we have opportunities to plant seeds of knowledge and understanding in people's lives. Often these are people we will not see again. Even though we may never know whether or not our seeds germinated, out of love we will go ahead and make the effort. Our own good fortune and spiritual understanding has been helped along the way by people who took this risk out of love for us. Our responsibility is to keep the process going.

Experiment: Make special efforts to sow seeds of good in the lives of others. Do not be concerned whether or not you will be around to observe the results.

Chapter Twelve
SPIRIT

"What are the relationships among such terms as: The spirit of the times, the spirit of the age. . .the Spirit of the Christ, the SPIRIT OF GOD?" p. 107

These are exciting times in which to be alive. The potential for spiritual breakthrough on the planet may be greater than at any time since the life of Jesus. There are tremendous influences building up to thrust human consciousness over a threshold into a new age. Each of us can get with the spirit of these times and help in the birthing process of a new human awareness. The first step in cooperating with the spirit of transition is to recognize what impact it is having right now on individuals and on the nation. There are at least four significant components of this spirit:

(1) *The spirit of change* is evident everywhere we look. In some instances that spirit is misunderstood and it is used in a way which does not necessarily aid in the building of a new world. Manufactured goods force us to change when they are built with planned obsolescence. Some people want to change *everything* about our political and economic system because they have correctly found some of its weaknesses.

Nevertheless, when properly applied, the spirit of change is an aspect of the Spirit of God. Our universe is a dynamic, creative one; therefore, that which will not grow and evolve is doomed to die.

(2) *The spirit of rebirth* is a partner to the spirit of change. It affirms that even in the midst of continual change, there are some universal truths and universal laws which keep resurfacing. The spirit of rebirth has brought back an interest in the mystical roots of Christianity. It has made more and more people in the Western world interested in the concept of the soul's rebirth: reincarnation. The human personality can so

easily be ravaged by the effects of change that we need a complementary spirit—something which affirms an indestructible soul that can be reborn.

(3) *The spirit of polarization* is also evident in our times. This, too, is an expression of the Spirit of God. Yes, the oneness of God can sometimes express division *at the material level.* What did Jesus say? He came with a sword to divide. His teachings might set brother against brother. He would polarize things.

In our times the stress of change does the same thing. Stress either brings out the best in a person or the worst. The same is true of a nation or a world under stress.

(4) *The spirit of knowledge* is also a part of our times. Scientific knowledge is expanding at an almost inconceivable rate. But even more importantly, human knowledge of higher dimensions of reality is also expanding. The new age will be characterized by our knowledge of the Creative Forces and how these higher energies can be channeled and used in the material life. The following passage from the Cayce readings says just that:

Q-12. What will the Aquarian Age mean to mankind as regards physical, mental and spiritual development?...
A-12....the full consciousness of the ability to communicate with or to be aware of the relationships to the Creative Forces and the uses of same in material environs.

Then, as to what will these be—*only* those who accept same will even become aware of what's going on about them! How few realize the vibratory forces [that] create influences from even one individual to another...   1602-3

Our work is to recognize these four aspects of God's Spirit which are active in our changing world. We need to cooperate with the flow of their influence. We especially need to make sure that these aspects are *properly understood* and properly applied. Despite the obvious stress and turmoil created by the influence of this Spirit, the prospects of where it is leading us are quite *hopeful.* Let us always keep this in mind as we seek to serve humanity through the time of transition into a new world order.

Experiment: Be alert for signs of the spirit of our changing times. Try to act and think in such a way that you cooperate with and help to build a new world. Be especially aware of how to talk to others about the challenges and difficulties of the times. Let your words bespeak the consciousness of hope.

"All force is one force. It is man who brought diversity of expression and perception, and man through the Way must return to Unity." p. 107

So often in the *A Search for God* material we find the concept of oneness stressed. It is not just the first lesson in the development of spiritual awareness; it is a recurrent theme which has a role to play in all the other steps of our growth sequence.

The principle of oneness seems so straightforward and so readily grasped. Even modern science is moving toward a unified theory of energy and forces. Oneness has become *the* central point of religion and science. So if it is a principle so easily acceptable and so simple in structure, why do we continually come back to it? As you started to read this particular section, was your reaction, "Oh, here we go again on that stuff about oneness"? We think we have got it, so why keep dwelling on it?

The answer is that our intellectual minds easily accept the notion of oneness but our emotions and behaviors often do not. We say we believe in one force—in one God—but so often we do not act and react that way. In our own subtle ways we have an array of gods to represent the various different forms which the one force can take on.

You may be saying to yourself, "No, not me. I don't believe in many gods. There are no little statues or idols around my house." This may be true. However, each of us has found a different way to have many gods.

Think of it this way: A god (with a little "g") is a symbol which consistently awakens in you an automatic response at a *single* emotional level. For example, whenever the ancient Romans would look upon a statue of the god Mars they were expected to have a very specific emotional reaction. That reaction was the one force acting through the adrenal glands: a war-like, aggressive or angry feeling. Something is a god whenever that symbol—whatever it may be—consistently stimulates in us a *single* expression of the one force which is *only one of many possible expressions.*

Instead of statues, you and I have made *people* into our gods. Each of us has a few people in our lives who *always awaken the same emotional reaction* in us whenever we think of them. For example, whenever I think of Mr. Smith, I always feel anxious. Therefore, Mr. Smith has become a god for me: the god of anxiety. Whenever I think of Miss Anderson, I always feel disappointment. Her image has become a god of disappointment for me.

If we truly *believed* in one God (believed with our actions and feelings, too), then no person would always awaken in us a single emotional response. We would meet each situation anew, knowing that the one force *can* express as anxiety or disappointment, but *can also just as naturally* express as joy or love.

We need to identify who these people are whom we have made into gods. It is not a matter of whom we admire and idolize (that is the way we often use the phrase). Instead it is a matter of getting locked-in with a single way of using the one force in our relationship with that person.

Experiment: Whom have you made into a god in your life? For each person you can name, write down what single emotional reaction you have upon seeing or thinking about that person. Try exploring some different ways of reacting to each of those individuals. Rediscover that there really is just one force, although there are many ways you can use it in that relationship.

"In all states of consciousness there are opportunities for the expression of. . .[soul, mind and will]." p. 108

Have you ever said to yourself, "I'll get back to my spiritual work just as soon as this down period is over"? Have you identified certain states as the ones which *allow* you to grow and other states as ones which *prevent* growth? If so, then you have marked off a part of your life and decided that it is outside the domain of God's influence.

It is so easy for us to do this. Almost all of us have particular emotional or physical states which make it quite difficult to complete our spiritual disciplines or to keep a spiritual outlook on life. Our tendency is to label them as "out of bounds," as the areas which are infertile for any kind of development. We say to ourselves, to God and to others, "Just leave me alone when I am in this state; I could never do what you expect of me."

Yet we still may wonder why the Bible emphasizes God's omnipresence. Why does the Psalmist say words like these:

"Whither shall I go from thy Spirit? Or whither shall I flee from thy presence?

"If I ascend to heaven, thou art there! If I make my bed in Sheol, thou art there!" (Psalm 139:7-8)

Perhaps we are mistaken in our assumption that some ground of daily human experience is infertile. Perhaps the problem is the *expectations* we place on ourselves—the expectations which we assume that God and others *always* have for us. What happens is that we get caught up in the specific *form* of what our spiritual work looks like. But there are days when we do not have the energy or the patience to complete that array of activities. So, we end up labeling such periods as our times when we just are not going to grow.

We would be better off to revise our self-expectations. We could abandon for the day our *usual* form of spiritual growth and ask ourselves, "What little things *can* I do today?"

For example, suppose that Mr. A normally gets up to meditate from 6:30-7:00 a.m. and follows that with a two-mile jog. At his job he makes it a discipline to smile at a dozen different people each day. However, Monday morning he wakes up tired and in a bad mood. Does he decide that this is just not going to be a day when he can complete his usual physical/mental/spiritual program? Or does he *revise his expectations and meet himself at his own level?*

Mr. A *could* decide to have just a five-minute prayer period and jog half a mile. He might be able to muster only four or five smiles at work. And yet, as seen from the perspective of his soul, doing these scaled-down activities still may have led to just as much growth and development as any other day; or maybe more so, since he tried to do his best even when he "didn't feel like it."

Experiment: Remember each day that growth toward God can happen in whatever state or mood you find yourself. When you feel down, revise your expectations for yourself. Keep your efforts pointed in the *direction* of your idea, but take *smaller steps.*

"Step by step spiritual beings became aware that they were away from God, from Light." p. 108

The human soul is on a journey of consciousness. The journey is not toward some place or some time. Instead it is a movement toward a special kind of awareness. The destination is full consciousness of ourselves as children of God, full consciousness of God and knowledge of the relationship between the two. Our goal is to know ourselves to be ourselves and yet one with the whole—one with God.

So, the problematic aspect of living is one of becoming more conscious. If there is a force or influence in the universe which is trying to keep us apart from our spiritual destiny, then it must be something which works against greater consciousness. The so-called forces of evil are not so much those which make us do things we should not do. They are those influences which make us unconscious. Perhaps out of unconsciousness we do things we shouldn't do, but the problem must be tackled at its origin and not at the symptom level.

What does it mean to be unconscious? It is certainly far more than just a sleeplike or comatose state. We can be awake and functional yet still have a degree of unconsciousness about us. The mere *perception* of events is admittedly a kind of awareness, yet it does not insure consciousness. A computer can scan an environment and perceive conditions around it, yet no one is ready to call a computer conscious.

The essential ingredients of consciousness are: (1) a self-reflectiveness and (2) an awareness of free will. The computer can perceive data and analyze it; however, the computer is not self-reflective. Nor does the computer have awareness of free will. It responds to its own programming.

Too often we are like computers. We perceive what is happening—we take in data. However, it is wrong for us to assume that we are growing in consciousness just because we are aware of more information. If we do not remember ourselves—our spiritual ideals—then we are still in a relative state of unconsciousness. If we do not remember our own free will, then we merely react to our own karmic programming. We can walk through life with our eyes open yet still rather asleep. It has been a tragic mistake that so many people have assumed that mind-altering drugs would move them along faster on their spiritual journey. In fact these substances may be *awareness*-expanding but they are *not consciousness*-expanding.

Perhaps nocturnal dreaming provides one of the best illustrations of what we need to do in order to become more conscious. In a normal dream we have a kind of awareness which is expanded beyond our normal waking awareness. However, our consciousness is minimal. We have very little self-reflective capability in the normal dream. Primarily we simply react to what is happening in the dream story.

The dramatic exception to this is the lucid dream—in which we suddenly realize in the dream that we are dreaming. We have moved in consciousness at this point—we remember ourselves as an identity with life beyond this particular dream world. We also realize that we have free will—that we do not have to keep acting the way we have been in the dream.

Our journey in materiality requires us to learn to do something *analogous* to becoming lucid in a nocturnal dream. Whether or not we start having lucid dreams at night, we still need to begin remembering our real selves and our free will. We started out eons ago as one with God—aware of Him yet *not conscious* of our *individual* Godlike nature. The end of our journey will be re-establishing the awareness of God's presence, but this time with consciousness of who we are. It will be a conscious union instead of an unconscious one.

Experiment: Make it a discipline as many times as you can throughout the day to remember your real self. Take note of your free will. Continually try to move yourself from living as if you were in a dream to living as if you were truly conscious.

"...we will come to know ourselves to be ourselves, yet one with and part of the whole, yet not the Whole. That is the purpose, that is the cause, of Being." p. 108

In the previous experiment we explored the foundations of this quote from *A Search for God.* Our journey in consciousness is to develop simultaneously real self-identity *and* transpersonal identity. As paradoxical as this may sound, it is the way great spiritual teachers have described it for centuries.

But we may wonder where we begin in our attempt to develop such an awareness of being one with the Whole. The answer is in the human relationships we have with those around us. There is no better ground on which to meet the divine than in our interactions with others. We can learn about and discover the process of *cosmic* unity in the *microcosmic* arena of interpersonal relations.

A good place to begin is with a small group of people. It may be your family, it may be your study group or your group at work. In selecting twelve apostles Jesus seemed to be advocating the small group as an especially productive format of raising consciousness. Your group may be as small as two people or as large as Jesus' group of apostles.

In the small group *working together harmoniously for a common ideal,* we can have an experience of *group consciousness.* We will have moments—perhaps only brief—in which we realize that there is an energy and even a consciousness that is "us." The individuals of that group are one with this newly created identity but they also retain their individuality. It is what we might call "trans-individual consciousness"— consciousness of something beyond our individual nature. For example, in the diagram below, six squares come together and form a cube. Each square retains its identity but is also one with a newly created *and higher dimensional* identity.

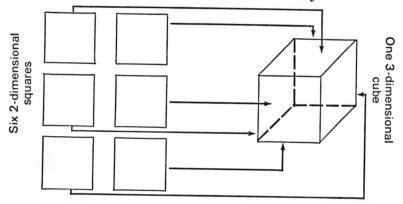

How can we foster this kind of group consciousness experience in the groups to which we already belong? Our efforts can be in each of the three elements used previously to describe group consciousness.

(1) A *common ideal* is required. We can help the group clarify for itself a purpose and make sure that is clearly understood by all group members. What are we about? What makes us want to be together and what are we trying to do with our togetherness?

(2) *Harmony* and cooperation allow the group consciousness to emerge. Each part must support the other. We can foster better communication among group members. We can by our own example of cooperation stimulate greater harmony among all group members.

(3) *Working together* is a necessary ingredient. That is, our groups must be actively involved in *doing something* if group consciousness is to emerge. Get your family working on a project together (e.g., home improvement, gardening, recreation, etc.). Get your study group involved in a service project or in helping a new group get started. People who sit around and *just* talk or *just* watch television are not going to experience group consciousness.

Experiment: Pick one group of which you are a member. Do your part to apply the three ingredients of fostering transindividual group consciousness.

"Every day is the awareness of the evening and the morning being the first day. . .Every moment we are just beginning to live." p. 110

There is great wisdom in a common, overworked phrase: "Today is the first day of the rest of my life." It expresses the uniqueness of this day and the freshness of each morning. It can also be understood to reflect the love and forgiveness of God. What is past is past. Having put my hand to the plow, this morning I need not look back, because all that God asks of me is to go forward with the right spirit.

There is a healing that happens in the night. As we sleep and dream, the cares and problems of the previous day are being worked on. So often when we awaken in the morning, there is the opportunity to adopt a whole new point of view toward some difficulty from yesterday. Unfortunately we sometimes miss that opportunity. Often we automatically and unconsciously step back into the same old feeling or attitude.

The first five or ten minutes of a new day are crucial ones. They can set the tone for the following 16 hours or so of waking life. There is an opportunity in those first few minutes to get your life oriented and focused. There is the opportunity to receive the healing—which may have been incubated during the night—of some problem.

Even if you are not a "morning person," you can still work with this principle. It does not mean that you have to get right out of bed and go jogging or have a long meditation period. What is needed is something we all can do upon awakening. In those first few moments of the morning feel the freshness, promise and new beginnings which the day offers. Feel a sense of openness to accept any healing which may have occurred in the night. And then say a short prayer thanking God for this day and dedicating the day to your ideal of love and service.

Experiment: Use the first few minutes of each new day to get started with the right consciousness.

"Is God not the God of the heaven, the universe? Should He not be God of the nation. . .What moves us to find fault with our brother, to cause inharmonies. . .in the nation?" p. 111

America has a rich heritage of spirituality. Its foundation—built more than 200 years ago—was created by many people who had an understanding of metaphysics and spiritual law. We need only look at the symbology of the Great Seal of the United States (particularly the reverse side, which can be found on a dollar bill) to get the feeling that the nation was founded for spiritual as well as political reasons.

The Cayce readings indicate that in these times of testing on the earth, America has a particularly important role to play in worldwide spiritual leadership. The following reading refers to President Wilson at the peace talks following World War I. It also warns that if our nation does not fulfill the opportunities of these times, the mantle of spiritual leadership will move westward—presumably to the Orient.

The spirituality of the American people will be rather as the criterion of that as is to become the world's forces, for, as has been given in that of the peace table, there sat the Master in the American people, with the brotherhood of the world accepted—war was at an end. Without same there will again come the Armageddon, and in same there will be seen that the Christian forces will *again* move westward. 900-272

To take pride in our nation does not necessarily mean narrow-minded nationalism. Nor does it mean to condone the many failings of the American people or to approve of the actions of our government. America is the spirit of our people and the ideals upon which it was founded. Instead of looking to Washington, D.C., or our state capitol for a symbol of America, let us look to ourselves. To what extent are *we* living the ideals upon which our nation was created? These ideals include respect for the freedom and responsibility of each individual; faith in God; and unity out of diversity.

We can each work to make our nation strong in purpose. This comes from living the ideals set at our country's inception. It comes from positive thinking and finding supportive statements to make. The tendency today is to take the easy way out. It is far simpler to criticize our fellow countrymen. It is easy to blame our problems on a government which did not give us what we wanted. Yes, government may need to change, but— keep in mind—it *reflects* the consciousness of its people; it doesn't *create* the consciousness. In these times—more than any in many years—is needed an America which is harmonious and refocused on its original ideals.

Experiment: Observe how you think and speak about this country and its leaders. Take responsibility yourself for living more fully some of the ideals upon which the nation was founded.

" 'Is it possible, I thought, that true rest comes from the realization of a selfless life?' " p. 111

There are at least two distinct ways in which we use up energy and get tired. One is through physical activity and the other is through stress. We know the kind of tiredness which comes on a day when we have worked hard but joyfully. Even when we really enjoy what we are doing, there comes a point at which the body needs rest and a period for renewal. We may say, "I feel tired, but it is a good kind of tired."

However, the tiredness which comes from stress is of a different sort. Stress is a physical experience. Although it usually originates in the mind, it operates on and depletes the physical body. This type of tiredness will usually arise more quickly because energy is being used to get work done *and* to compensate for the effects of the stress.

Take a moment and consider how your energy level has been lately. It is an often quoted figure that humans may use only 10% of their mental potential. What percentage of your energy level *potential* do you suppose you make available to yourself each day? How much energy do you suppose you draw upon and use each day in actually getting work done? To what degree do you suppose that worry, anxiety, tension or any other form of stress cuts you off from greater storehouses of energy? You can change these figures for your life. You know how to do it because, no doubt, you have had the experience before.

The key is to replace the stress. Its best replacement is its opposite—harmony with one's ideal. That is to say, when you can live with a sense of harmony with your ideal, there will be an optimum experience of your energy level. You may find that you need less sleep and that you feel focused and energized throughout the day.

For most of us our ideal is *a life of serving and loving others.* As we spend extra time serving and doing good to help others—instead of worrying or being anxious—we will have more energy than we ever had before. We will not experience a need to rest so often. In fact, sometimes we will experience the acts of service as restful and reenergizing in themselves. Perhaps this is what the Christ's invitation meant—to come unto Him and find rest.

Experiment: Take note of what your energy levels have tended to be like for the last few weeks. Then try to spend a little more time each day (perhaps only 30 minutes) in sincere and loving service to someone. Observe whether or not this new activity seems to (a) drain energy, (b) create new energy but still not drain any, or (c) reenergize you, renew and rest you.

" *'I was looking down on a most beautiful, broad river, composed of flowing bubbles. . .I realized that the bubbles were PEOPLE! They, the bubbles, finally reached a place where they burst, and all seemed to be one.' "* p. 112

What is it about material possessions and riches which can get in the way of our knowing God? Why did Jesus say that it was easier for a camel to pass through the eye of a needle than for a rich man to enter into the kingdom of heaven? There is nothing in itself wrong with a material possession or access to resources (which money symbolizes). And yet, even when we recognize that God is the source of all supply, even when we thank Him for riches, they can still create a problem for us.

The reason for this is multifaceted, but perhaps the heart of the issue is this: Material wealth creates a strong influence to put *things before people*. In the extreme case, imagine the example of a family of great wealth with a nice home, several new cars and many rare antiques. Their tendency may be preoccupation with how to protect those possessions. And they may be quite correct in assuming that there are people who might desire to steal from them what they have. Nevertheless, it may still create a tension between them and other people.

However, you may be saying: "I'm not rich that way. I don't live in fear of being robbed." But are there other ways in which you put *things before people?* Take a moment and see if you observe this tendency in any form within your own thoughts and actions.

Perhaps you will find that you have a very good handle on this potential problem—that almost always you put other people's feelings and needs before your own material possessions. But be sure to consider also another, more subtle form of this same process. We may occasionally put before people our own ideas or our own intentions to get something accomplished. For example, we may get so attached to the idea of how something ought to be done that the idea becomes more important to us than do the people around us. Or we may get up such a head of steam to get something accomplished that we run roughshod over people to get it done.

However, *people* and relationships are our work. That is really all that matters. Certainly we cannot go through life accommodating others in their every whim and desire. There are times when out of love and commitment to an ideal we say, "No, I cannot do for you what you want." But in such instances there can be a strong *awareness* of love which motivates what we are doing. We *can* put *people before things* and yet still say "no" to people sometimes. What is needed is merely clear priorities for our concern.

People are our work. One of Jesus' last instructions was "Feed my lambs; feed my sheep." Let us be careful not to let material goods or any narrow-minded compulsiveness get in the way of putting the feelings and needs of other people first in our lives.

Experiment: Put concern and love for people first in your life. Try being with people and really *enjoying* their company and the sharing and love which is possible in being together.

THE EDGAR CAYCE LEGACIES

Among the vast resources which have grown out of the late Edgar Cayce's work are:

The Readings: Available for examination and study at the Association for Research and Enlightenment, Inc.,(A.R.E.®) at Virginia Beach, Va., are 14,256 readings consisting of 49,135 pages of verbatim psychic material plus related correspondence. The readings are the clairvoyant discourses given by Cayce while he was in a self-induced hypnotic sleep-state. These discourses were recorded in shorthand and then typed. Copious indexing and cross-indexing make the readings readily accessible for study.

Research and Information: Medical information which flowed through Cayce is being researched and applied by the research divisions of the Edgar Cayce Foundation. Work is also being done with dreams and other aspects of ESP. Much information is disseminated through the A.R.E. Press publications, *A.R.E. News* and *The A.R.E. Journal.* Coordination of a nationwide program of lectures and conferences is in the hands of the Department of Education. A library specializing in psychic literature is available to the public with books on loan to members. An extensive tape library has A.R.E. lectures available for purchase. Resource material has been made available for authors, resulting in the publication of scores of books, booklets and other material.

A.R.E. Study Groups: The Edgar Cayce material is most valuable when worked with in an A.R.E. Study Group, the text for which is *A Search for God,* Books I and II. These books are the outcome of eleven years of work by Edgar Cayce with the first A.R.E. group and represent the distillation of wisdom which flowed through him in the trance condition. Hundreds of A.R.E. groups flourish throughout the United States and other countries. Their primary purpose is to assist the members to know their relationship to their Creator and to become channels of love and service to others. The groups are nondenominational and avoid ritual and dogma. There are no dues or fees required to join a group although contributions may be accepted.

Membership: A.R.E. has an open-membership policy which offers attractive benefits.

For more information write A.R.E., Box 595, Virginia Beach, Va. 23451. To obtain information about publications, please direct your query to A.R.E. Press. To obtain information about joining or perhaps starting an A.R.E. Study Group, please direct your letter to the Study Group Department.